# Wisher

## VOLUME 1 - NIGEL

ARTWORK

**GIULIO DE VITA**

SCRIPT

**SEBASTIEN LATOUR**

COLOURS

**EMANUELE TENDERINI**

9th CINEBOOK
The 9th Art Publisher

Original title: Nigel

Original edition: Editions du Lombard (Dargaud – Lombard s.a.) 2008
by De Vita & Latour
www.lelombard.com
All rights reserved

English translation: © 2013 Cinebook Ltd

Translator: Mark Bence
Lettering and text layout: Design Amorandi
Printed in Spain by Just Colour Graphic

This edition first published in Great Britain in 2014 by
Cinebook Ltd
56 Beech Avenue
Canterbury, Kent
CT4 7TA
www.cinebook.com

A CIP catalogue record for this book
is available from the British Library

ISBN 978-1-84918-215-7

9th CINEBOOK
The 9th Art Publisher

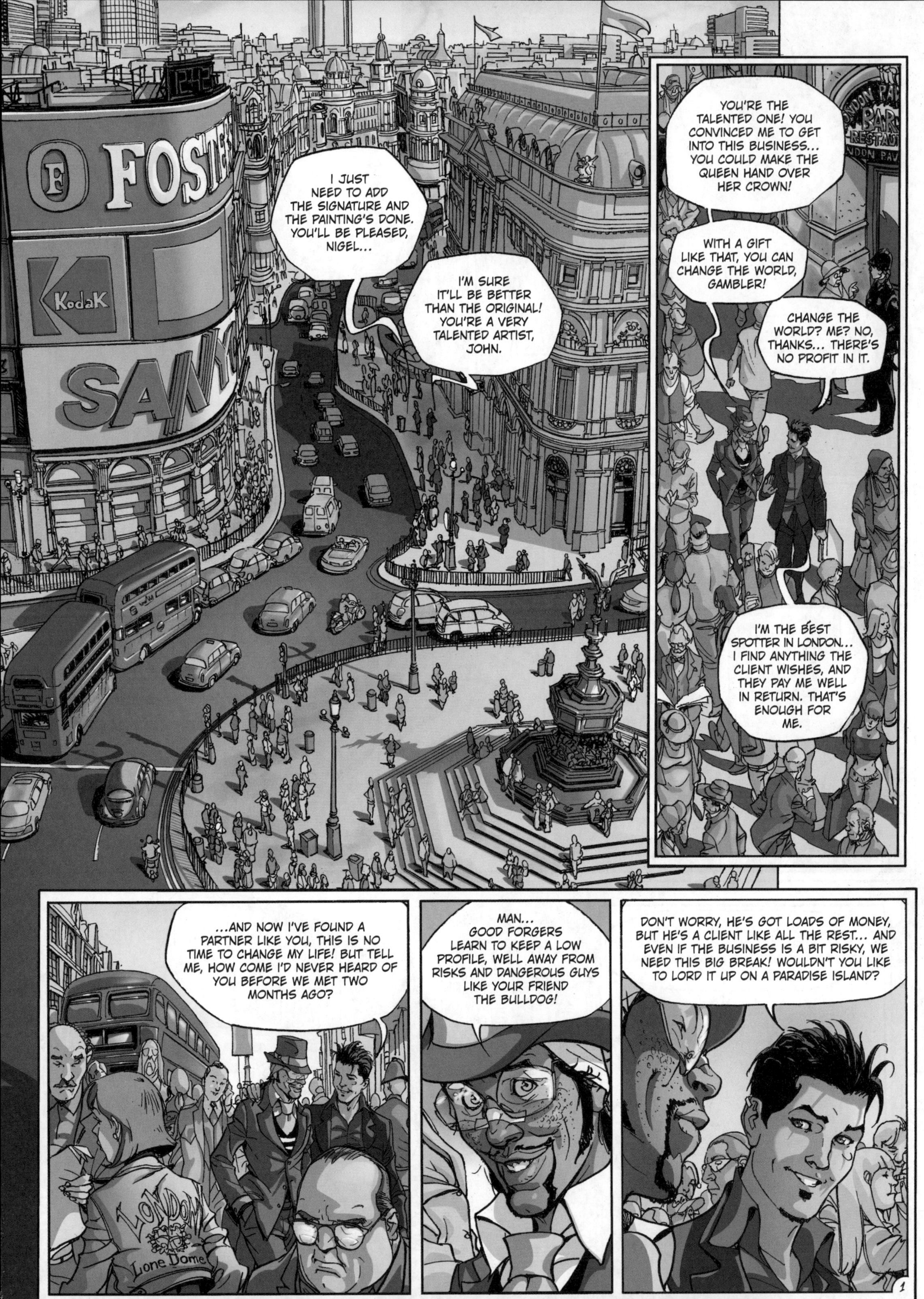

I JUST NEED TO ADD THE SIGNATURE AND THE PAINTING'S DONE. YOU'LL BE PLEASED, NIGEL...
I'M SURE IT'LL BE BETTER THAN THE ORIGINAL! YOU'RE A VERY TALENTED ARTIST, JOHN.
YOU'RE THE TALENTED ONE! YOU CONVINCED ME TO GET INTO THIS BUSINESS... YOU COULD MAKE THE QUEEN HAND OVER HER CROWN!
WITH A GIFT LIKE THAT, YOU CAN CHANGE THE WORLD, GAMBLER!
CHANGE THE WORLD? ME? NO, THANKS... THERE'S NO PROFIT IN IT.
I'M THE BEST SPOTTER IN LONDON... I FIND ANYTHING THE CLIENT WISHES, AND THEY PAY ME WELL IN RETURN. THAT'S ENOUGH FOR ME.
...AND NOW I'VE FOUND A PARTNER LIKE YOU, THIS IS NO TIME TO CHANGE MY LIFE! BUT TELL ME, HOW COME I'D NEVER HEARD OF YOU BEFORE WE MET TWO MONTHS AGO?
MAN... GOOD FORGERS LEARN TO KEEP A LOW PROFILE, WELL AWAY FROM RISKS AND DANGEROUS GUYS LIKE YOUR FRIEND THE BULLDOG!
DON'T WORRY, HE'S GOT LOADS OF MONEY, BUT HE'S A CLIENT LIKE ALL THE REST... AND EVEN IF THE BUSINESS IS A BIT RISKY, WE NEED THIS BIG BREAK! WOULDN'T YOU LIKE TO LORD IT UP ON A PARADISE ISLAND?

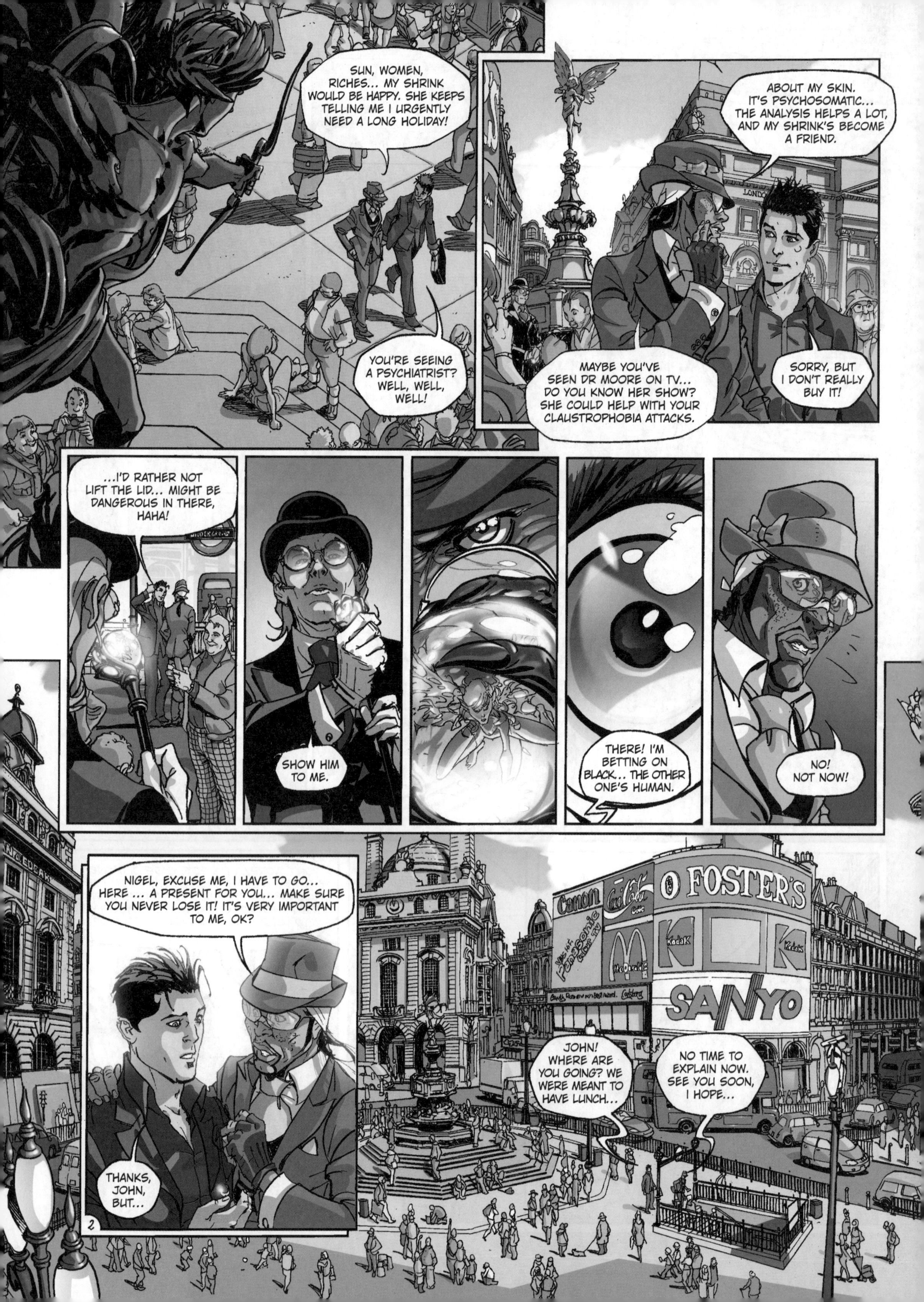

SUN, WOMEN, RICHES... MY SHRINK WOULD BE HAPPY. SHE KEEPS TELLING ME I URGENTLY NEED A LONG HOLIDAY!
YOU'RE SEEING A PSYCHIATRIST? WELL, WELL, WELL!
ABOUT MY SKIN. IT'S PSYCHOSOMATIC... THE ANALYSIS HELPS A LOT, AND MY SHRINK'S BECOME A FRIEND.
MAYBE YOU'VE SEEN DR MOORE ON TV... DO YOU KNOW HER SHOW? SHE COULD HELP WITH YOUR CLAUSTROPHOBIA ATTACKS.
SORRY, BUT I DON'T REALLY BUY IT!
...I'D RATHER NOT LIFT THE LID... MIGHT BE DANGEROUS IN THERE, HAHA!
SHOW HIM TO ME.
THERE! I'M BETTING ON BLACK... THE OTHER ONE'S HUMAN.
NO! NOT NOW!
NIGEL, EXCUSE ME, I HAVE TO GO... HERE ... A PRESENT FOR YOU... MAKE SURE YOU NEVER LOSE IT! IT'S VERY IMPORTANT TO ME, OK?
THANKS, JOHN, BUT...
JOHN! WHERE ARE YOU GOING? WE WERE MEANT TO HAVE LUNCH...
NO TIME TO EXPLAIN NOW. SEE YOU SOON, I HOPE...
FOSTER'S
SANYO

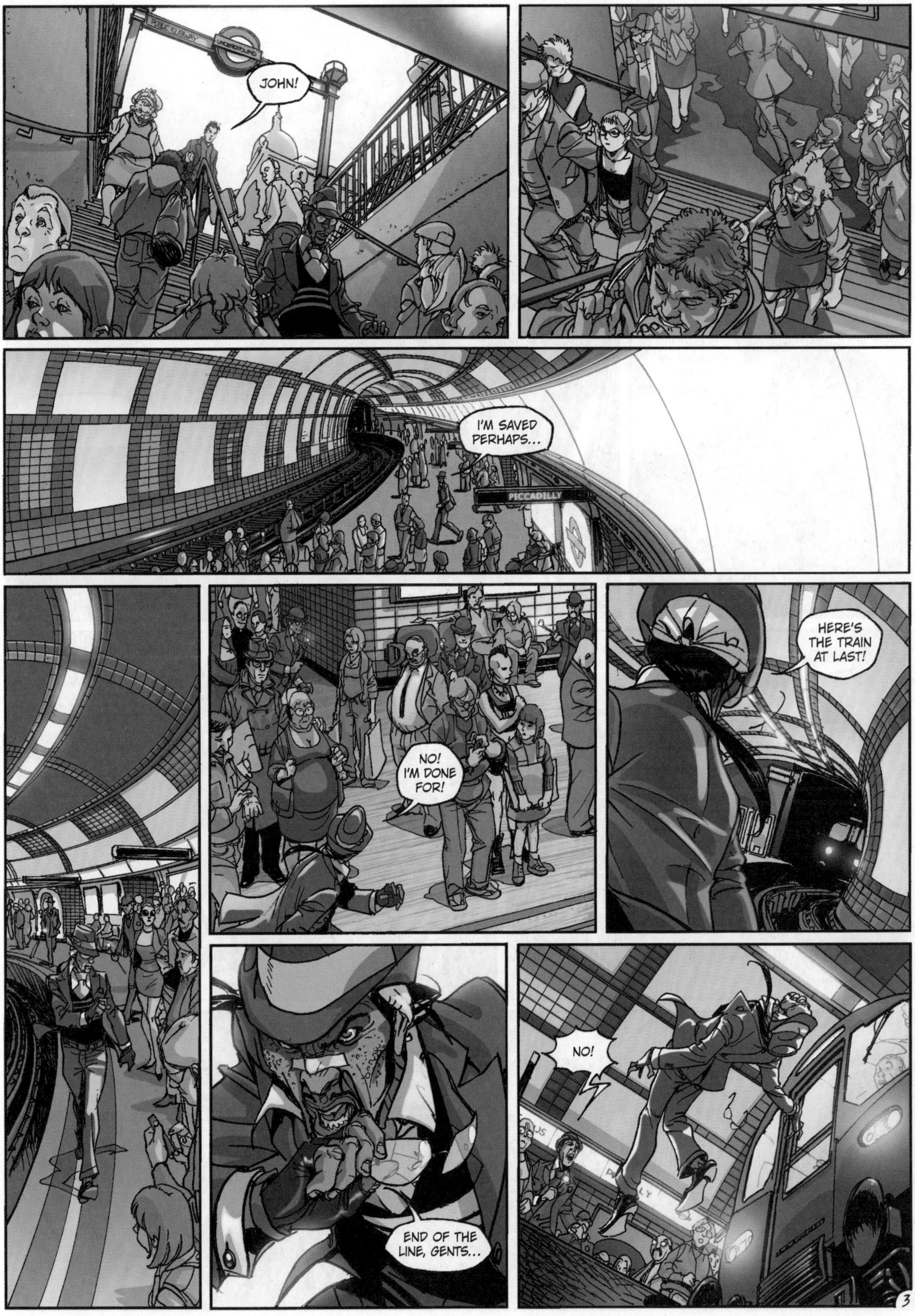
PUBLIC SUBWAY
UNDERGROUND
JOHN!
I'M SAVED PERHAPS...
PICCADILLY
NO! I'M DONE FOR!
HERE'S THE TRAIN AT LAST!
END OF THE LINE, GENTS...
NO!
3

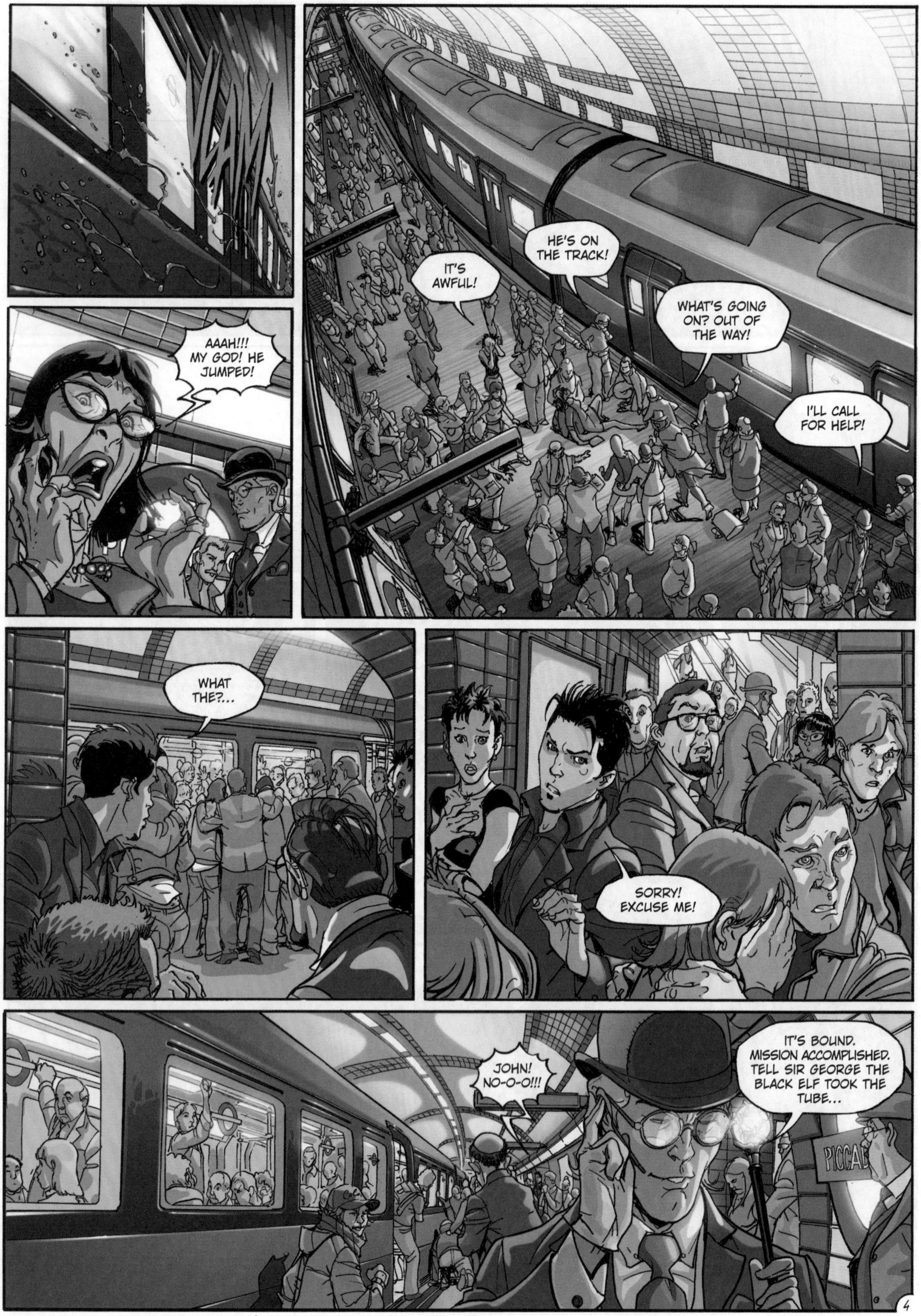
AAAH!!! MY GOD! HE JUMPED!
IT'S AWFUL!
HE'S ON THE TRACK!
WHAT'S GOING ON? OUT OF THE WAY!
I'LL CALL FOR HELP!
WHAT THE?...
SORRY! EXCUSE ME!
JOHN! NO-O-O!!!
IT'S BOUND. MISSION ACCOMPLISHED. TELL SIR GEORGE THE BLACK ELF TOOK THE TUBE...
PICCAD

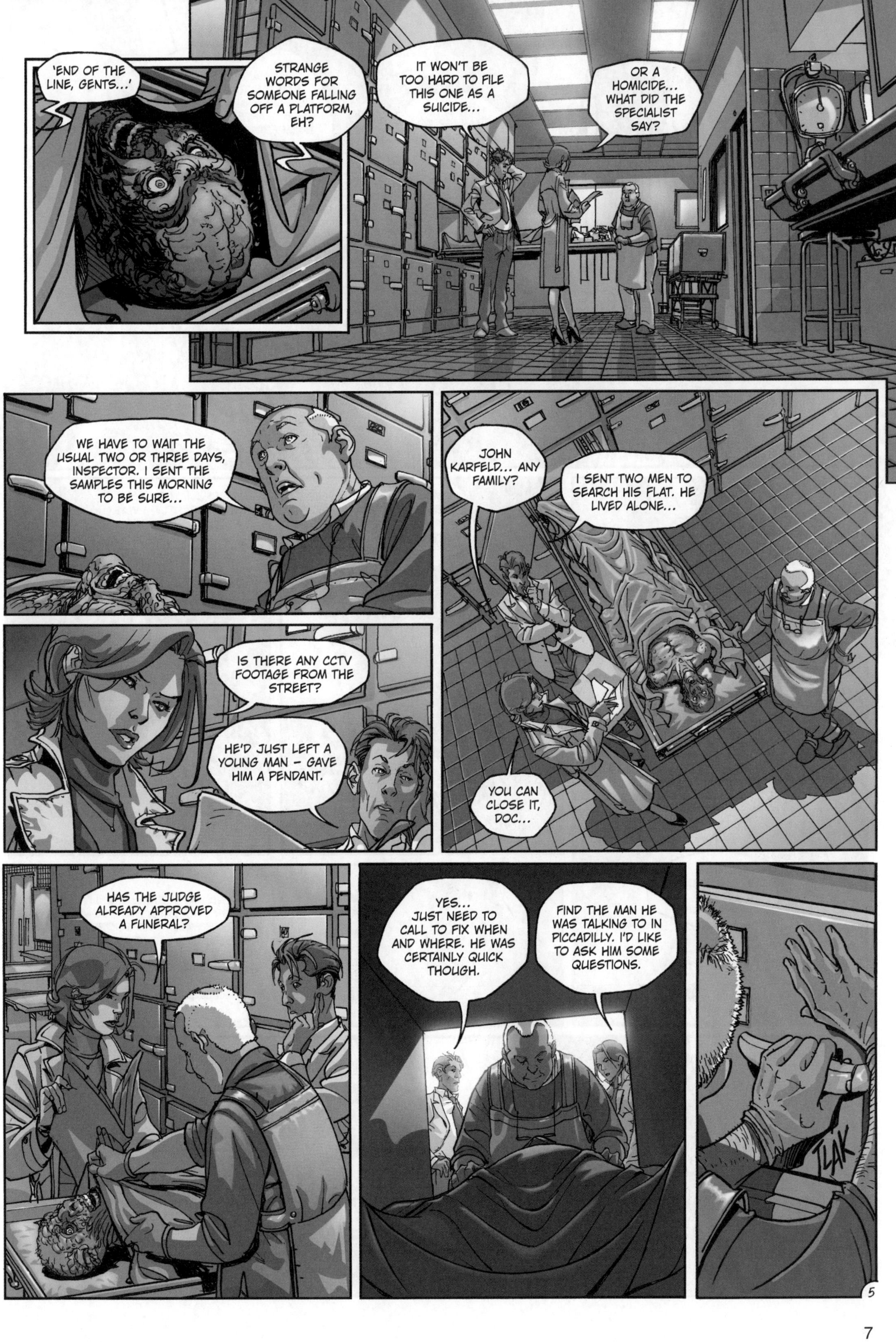
'END OF THE LINE, GENTS...'
STRANGE WORDS FOR SOMEONE FALLING OFF A PLATFORM, EH?
IT WON'T BE TOO HARD TO FILE THIS ONE AS A SUICIDE...
OR A HOMICIDE... WHAT DID THE SPECIALIST SAY?
WE HAVE TO WAIT THE USUAL TWO OR THREE DAYS, INSPECTOR. I SENT THE SAMPLES THIS MORNING TO BE SURE...
JOHN KARFELD... ANY FAMILY?
I SENT TWO MEN TO SEARCH HIS FLAT. HE LIVED ALONE...
IS THERE ANY CCTV FOOTAGE FROM THE STREET?
HE'D JUST LEFT A YOUNG MAN – GAVE HIM A PENDANT.
YOU CAN CLOSE IT, DOC...
HAS THE JUDGE ALREADY APPROVED A FUNERAL?
YES... JUST NEED TO CALL TO FIX WHEN AND WHERE. HE WAS CERTAINLY QUICK THOUGH.
FIND THE MAN HE WAS TALKING TO IN PICCADILLY. I'D LIKE TO ASK HIM SOME QUESTIONS.
TLAK
5

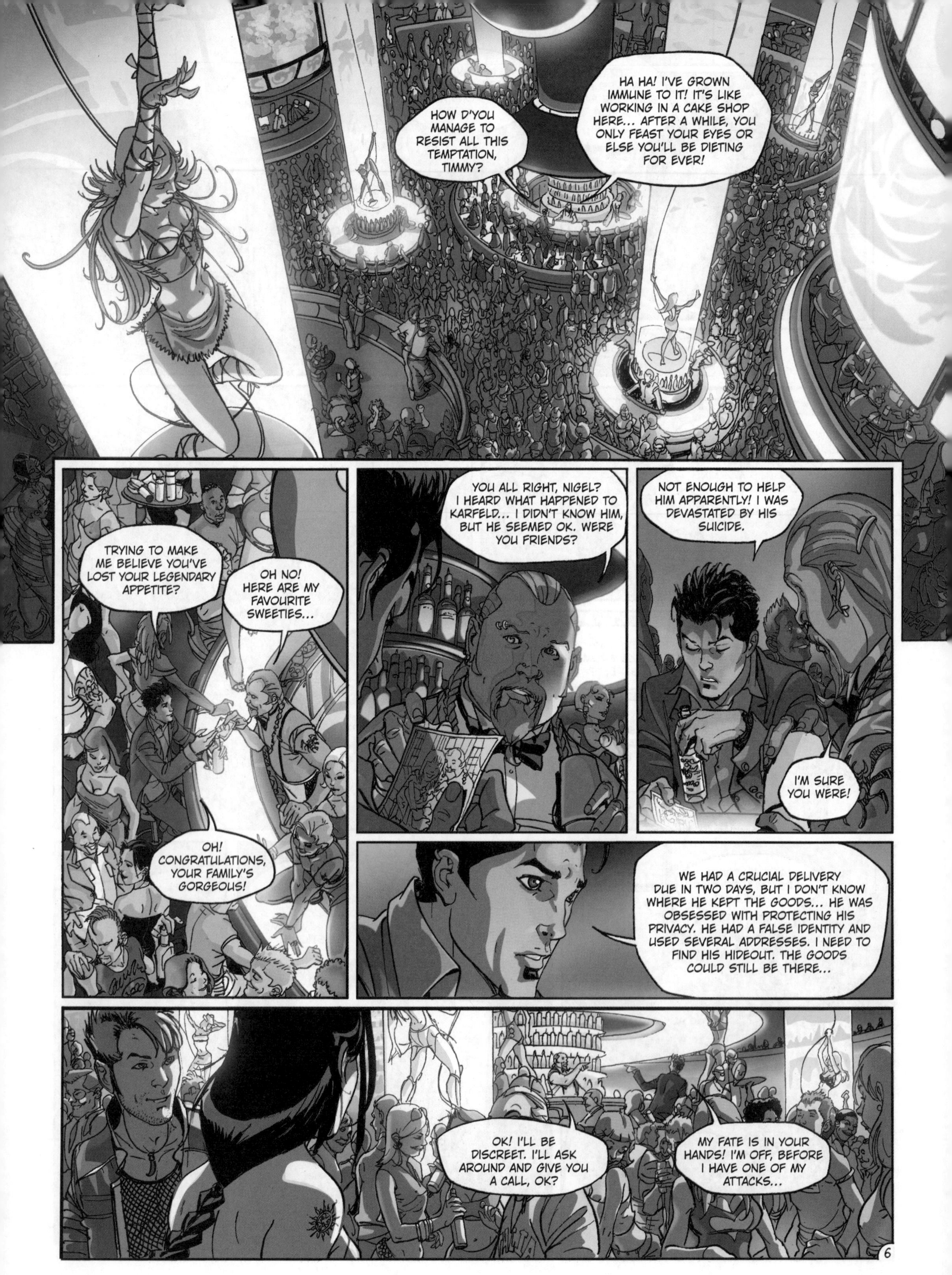
HOW D'YOU MANAGE TO RESIST ALL THIS TEMPTATION, TIMMY?
HA HA! I'VE GROWN IMMUNE TO IT! IT'S LIKE WORKING IN A CAKE SHOP HERE... AFTER A WHILE, YOU ONLY FEAST YOUR EYES OR ELSE YOU'LL BE DIETING FOR EVER!
TRYING TO MAKE ME BELIEVE YOU'VE LOST YOUR LEGENDARY APPETITE?
OH NO! HERE ARE MY FAVOURITE SWEETIES...
OH! CONGRATULATIONS, YOUR FAMILY'S GORGEOUS!
YOU ALL RIGHT, NIGEL? I HEARD WHAT HAPPENED TO KARFELD... I DIDN'T KNOW HIM, BUT HE SEEMED OK. WERE YOU FRIENDS?
NOT ENOUGH TO HELP HIM APPARENTLY! I WAS DEVASTATED BY HIS SUICIDE.
I'M SURE YOU WERE!
WE HAD A CRUCIAL DELIVERY DUE IN TWO DAYS, BUT I DON'T KNOW WHERE HE KEPT THE GOODS... HE WAS OBSESSED WITH PROTECTING HIS PRIVACY. HE HAD A FALSE IDENTITY AND USED SEVERAL ADDRESSES. I NEED TO FIND HIS HIDEOUT. THE GOODS COULD STILL BE THERE...
OK! I'LL BE DISCREET. I'LL ASK AROUND AND GIVE YOU A CALL, OK?
MY FATE IS IN YOUR HANDS! I'M OFF, BEFORE I HAVE ONE OF MY ATTACKS...
6

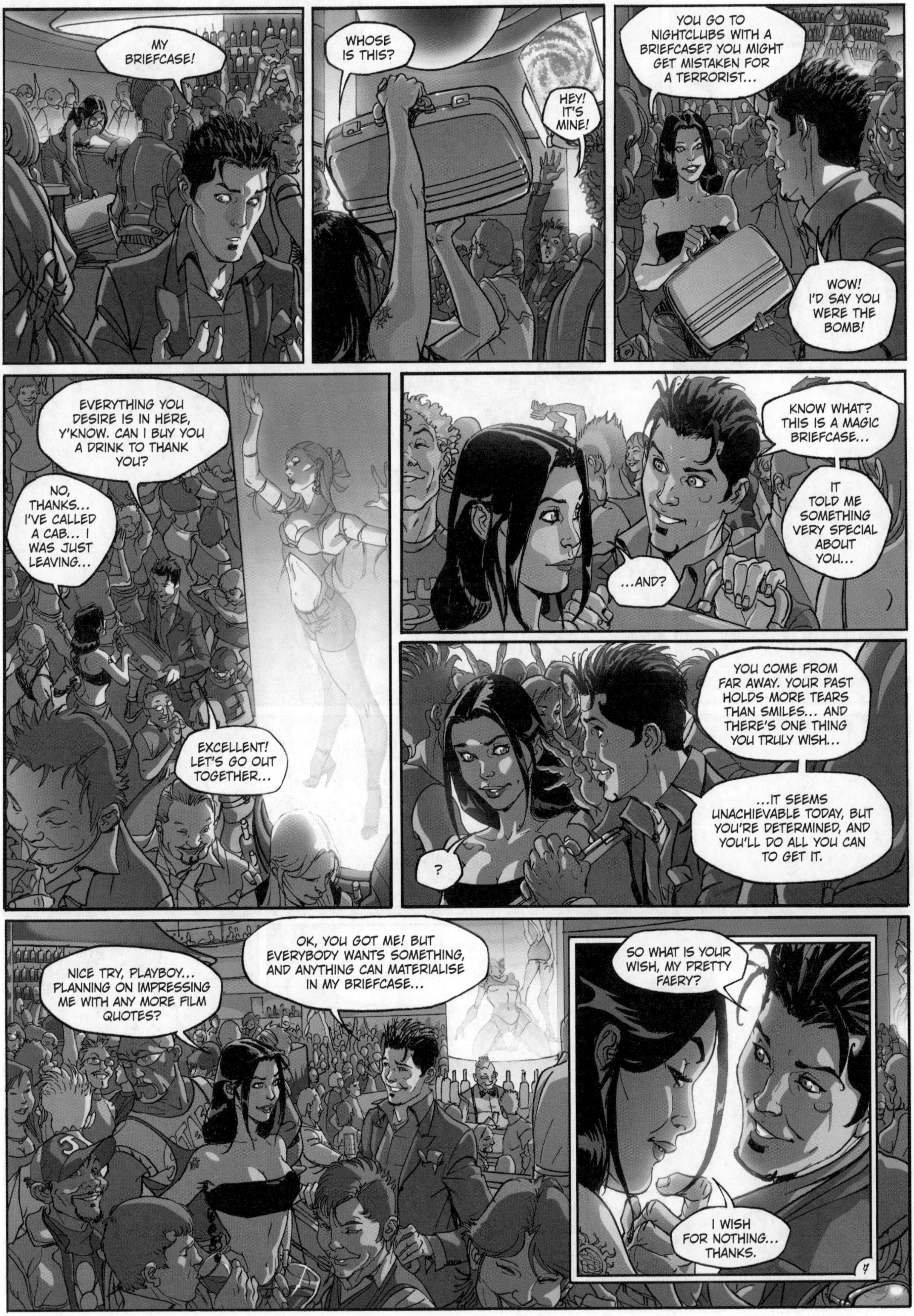

MY BRIEFCASE!
WHOSE IS THIS?
HEY! IT'S MINE!
YOU GO TO NIGHTCLUBS WITH A BRIEFCASE? YOU MIGHT GET MISTAKEN FOR A TERRORIST...
WOW! I'D SAY YOU WERE THE BOMB!
EVERYTHING YOU DESIRE IS IN HERE, Y'KNOW. CAN I BUY YOU A DRINK TO THANK YOU?
NO, THANKS... I'VE CALLED A CAB... I WAS JUST LEAVING...
EXCELLENT! LET'S GO OUT TOGETHER...
KNOW WHAT? THIS IS A MAGIC BRIEFCASE...
IT TOLD ME SOMETHING VERY SPECIAL ABOUT YOU...
...AND?
YOU COME FROM FAR AWAY. YOUR PAST HOLDS MORE TEARS THAN SMILES... AND THERE'S ONE THING YOU TRULY WISH...
...IT SEEMS UNACHIEVABLE TODAY, BUT YOU'RE DETERMINED, AND YOU'LL DO ALL YOU CAN TO GET IT.
?
NICE TRY, PLAYBOY... PLANNING ON IMPRESSING ME WITH ANY MORE FILM QUOTES?
OK, YOU GOT ME! BUT EVERYBODY WANTS SOMETHING, AND ANYTHING CAN MATERIALISE IN MY BRIEFCASE...
SO WHAT IS YOUR WISH, MY PRETTY FAERY?
I WISH FOR NOTHING... THANKS.

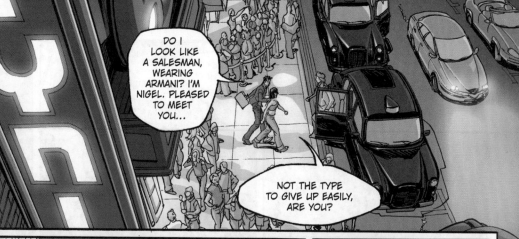

DO I LOOK LIKE A SALESMAN, WEARING ARMANI? I'M NIGEL. PLEASED TO MEET YOU...

NOT THE TYPE TO GIVE UP EASILY, ARE YOU?

YOU'RE THE FIRST PERSON I'VE MET WHO RADIATES HAPPINESS WITHOUT DEMANDING MORE! IT MAKES YOU INCREDIBLY FASCINATING.

YOU'RE IMPROVING ... BUT YOU TALK LIKE YOU'VE GOT SOMETHING TO SELL.

NO, I'M NOT... SO, WHAT'S YOUR NAME?

TO VALUE VICTORY, YOU SOMETIMES NEED TO TASTE DEFEAT, NIGEL...

GOODNIGHT THEN, NAMELESS ANGEL... TILL WE MEET AGAIN?

GOODNIGHT, NIGEL...

YOU REALLY WANT TO TAKE THIS TAXI!? I COULD DRIVE YOU IN MY...

YES, I'M TAKING THE TAXI.

WOW! WHAT A BEAUTY!

YOU DON'T WASTE ANY TIME, NIGEL...

BUT THEN, YOU'VE ALWAYS HAD GOOD TASTE IN VICTIMS!

JENNY? YOU, HERE?

...SHE KNOWS ALL ABOUT MANIPULATION TOO. BUT UNLIKE YOU, SHE DOESN'T BREAK HEARTS...

YOU KNOW HER?

I SEE HER EVERY TUESDAY. KNOW WHAT I WANT IN EXCHANGE FOR THAT INFORMATION?

SORRY, JENNY, BUT WHEN I BREAK UP WITH SOMEONE, IT'S PERMANENT.

8

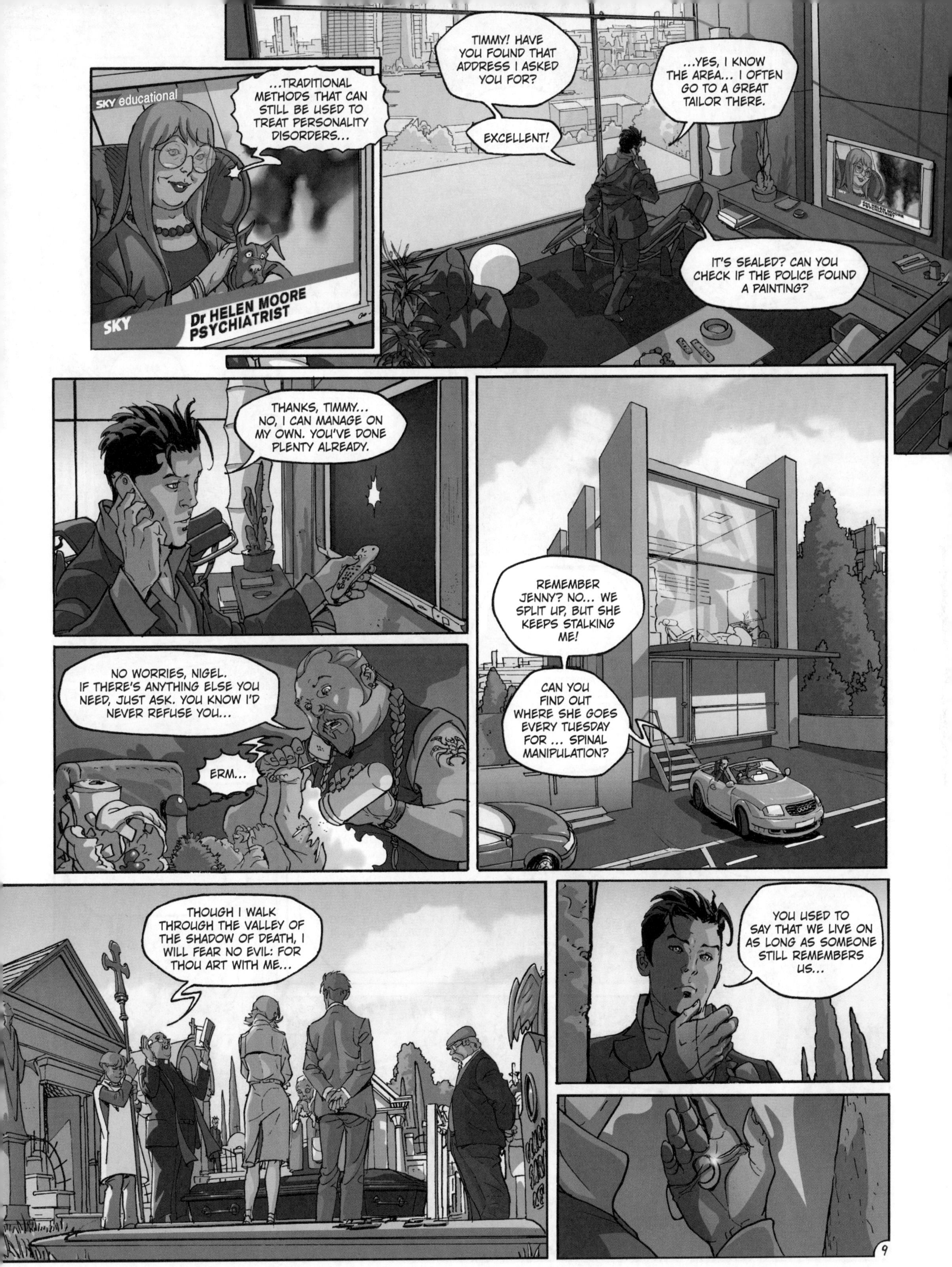
SKY educational
...TRADITIONAL METHODS THAT CAN STILL BE USED TO TREAT PERSONALITY DISORDERS...
Dr HELEN MOORE PSYCHIATRIST
SKY
TIMMY! HAVE YOU FOUND THAT ADDRESS I ASKED YOU FOR?
EXCELLENT!
...YES, I KNOW THE AREA... I OFTEN GO TO A GREAT TAILOR THERE.
IT'S SEALED? CAN YOU CHECK IF THE POLICE FOUND A PAINTING?
THANKS, TIMMY... NO, I CAN MANAGE ON MY OWN. YOU'VE DONE PLENTY ALREADY.
NO WORRIES, NIGEL. IF THERE'S ANYTHING ELSE YOU NEED, JUST ASK. YOU KNOW I'D NEVER REFUSE YOU...
ERM...
REMEMBER JENNY? NO... WE SPLIT UP, BUT SHE KEEPS STALKING ME!
CAN YOU FIND OUT WHERE SHE GOES EVERY TUESDAY FOR ... SPINAL MANIPULATION?
THOUGH I WALK THROUGH THE VALLEY OF THE SHADOW OF DEATH, I WILL FEAR NO EVIL: FOR THOU ART WITH ME...
YOU USED TO SAY THAT WE LIVE ON AS LONG AS SOMEONE STILL REMEMBERS US...
9

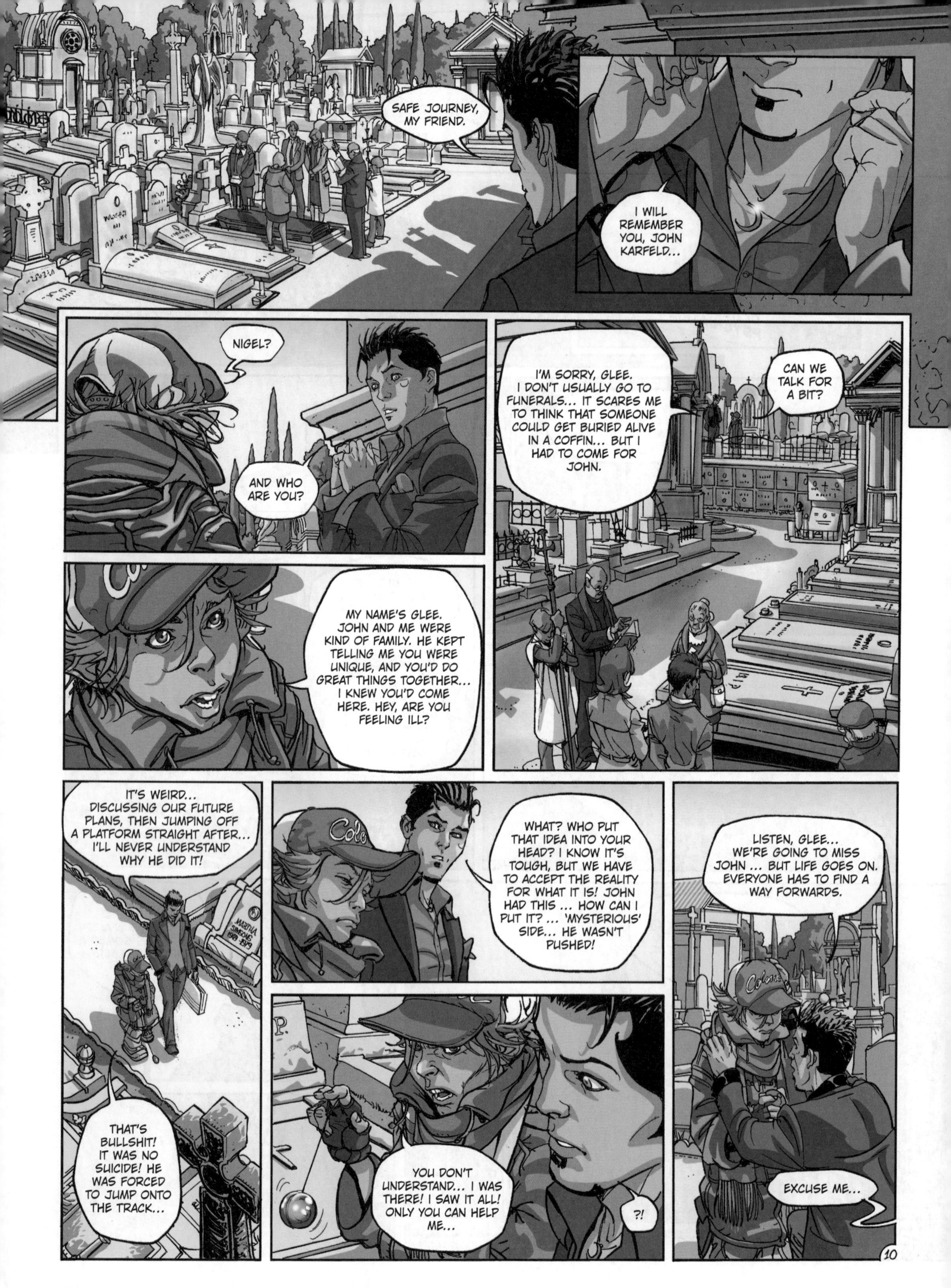
SAFE JOURNEY, MY FRIEND.
I WILL REMEMBER YOU, JOHN KARFELD...
NIGEL?
AND WHO ARE YOU?
I'M SORRY, GLEE. I DON'T USUALLY GO TO FUNERALS... IT SCARES ME TO THINK THAT SOMEONE COULD GET BURIED ALIVE IN A COFFIN... BUT I HAD TO COME FOR JOHN.
CAN WE TALK FOR A BIT?
MY NAME'S GLEE. JOHN AND ME WERE KIND OF FAMILY. HE KEPT TELLING ME YOU WERE UNIQUE, AND YOU'D DO GREAT THINGS TOGETHER... I KNEW YOU'D COME HERE. HEY, ARE YOU FEELING ILL?
IT'S WEIRD... DISCUSSING OUR FUTURE PLANS, THEN JUMPING OFF A PLATFORM STRAIGHT AFTER... I'LL NEVER UNDERSTAND WHY HE DID IT!
MARTHA SIMEONS 1913 1979
THAT'S BULLSHIT! IT WAS NO SUICIDE! HE WAS FORCED TO JUMP ONTO THE TRACK...
WHAT? WHO PUT THAT IDEA INTO YOUR HEAD? I KNOW IT'S TOUGH, BUT WE HAVE TO ACCEPT THE REALITY FOR WHAT IT IS! JOHN HAD THIS ... HOW CAN I PUT IT? ... 'MYSTERIOUS' SIDE... HE WASN'T PUSHED!
YOU DON'T UNDERSTAND... I WAS THERE! I SAW IT ALL! ONLY YOU CAN HELP ME...
?!
LISTEN, GLEE... WE'RE GOING TO MISS JOHN ... BUT LIFE GOES ON. EVERYONE HAS TO FIND A WAY FORWARDS.
EXCUSE ME...
10

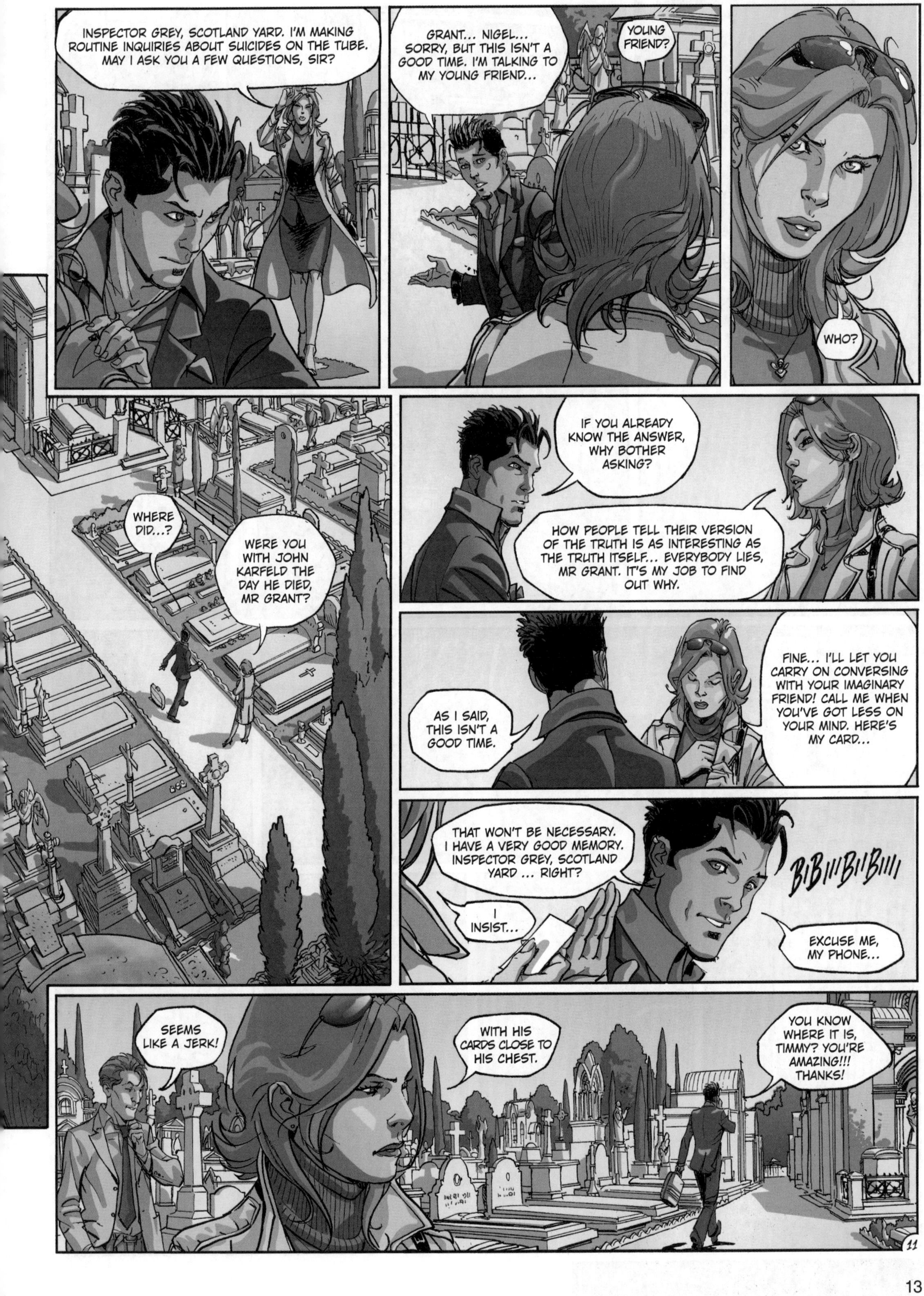
INSPECTOR GREY, SCOTLAND YARD. I'M MAKING ROUTINE INQUIRIES ABOUT SUICIDES ON THE TUBE. MAY I ASK YOU A FEW QUESTIONS, SIR?
GRANT... NIGEL... SORRY, BUT THIS ISN'T A GOOD TIME. I'M TALKING TO MY YOUNG FRIEND...
YOUNG FRIEND?
WHO?
WHERE DID...?
WERE YOU WITH JOHN KARFELD THE DAY HE DIED, MR GRANT?
IF YOU ALREADY KNOW THE ANSWER, WHY BOTHER ASKING?
HOW PEOPLE TELL THEIR VERSION OF THE TRUTH IS AS INTERESTING AS THE TRUTH ITSELF... EVERYBODY LIES, MR GRANT. IT'S MY JOB TO FIND OUT WHY.
FINE... I'LL LET YOU CARRY ON CONVERSING WITH YOUR IMAGINARY FRIEND! CALL ME WHEN YOU'VE GOT LESS ON YOUR MIND. HERE'S MY CARD...
AS I SAID, THIS ISN'T A GOOD TIME.
THAT WON'T BE NECESSARY. I HAVE A VERY GOOD MEMORY. INSPECTOR GREY, SCOTLAND YARD ... RIGHT?
I INSIST...
BIBIIIBIIBIIII
EXCUSE ME, MY PHONE...
SEEMS LIKE A JERK!
WITH HIS CARDS CLOSE TO HIS CHEST.
YOU KNOW WHERE IT IS, TIMMY? YOU'RE AMAZING!!! THANKS!
11

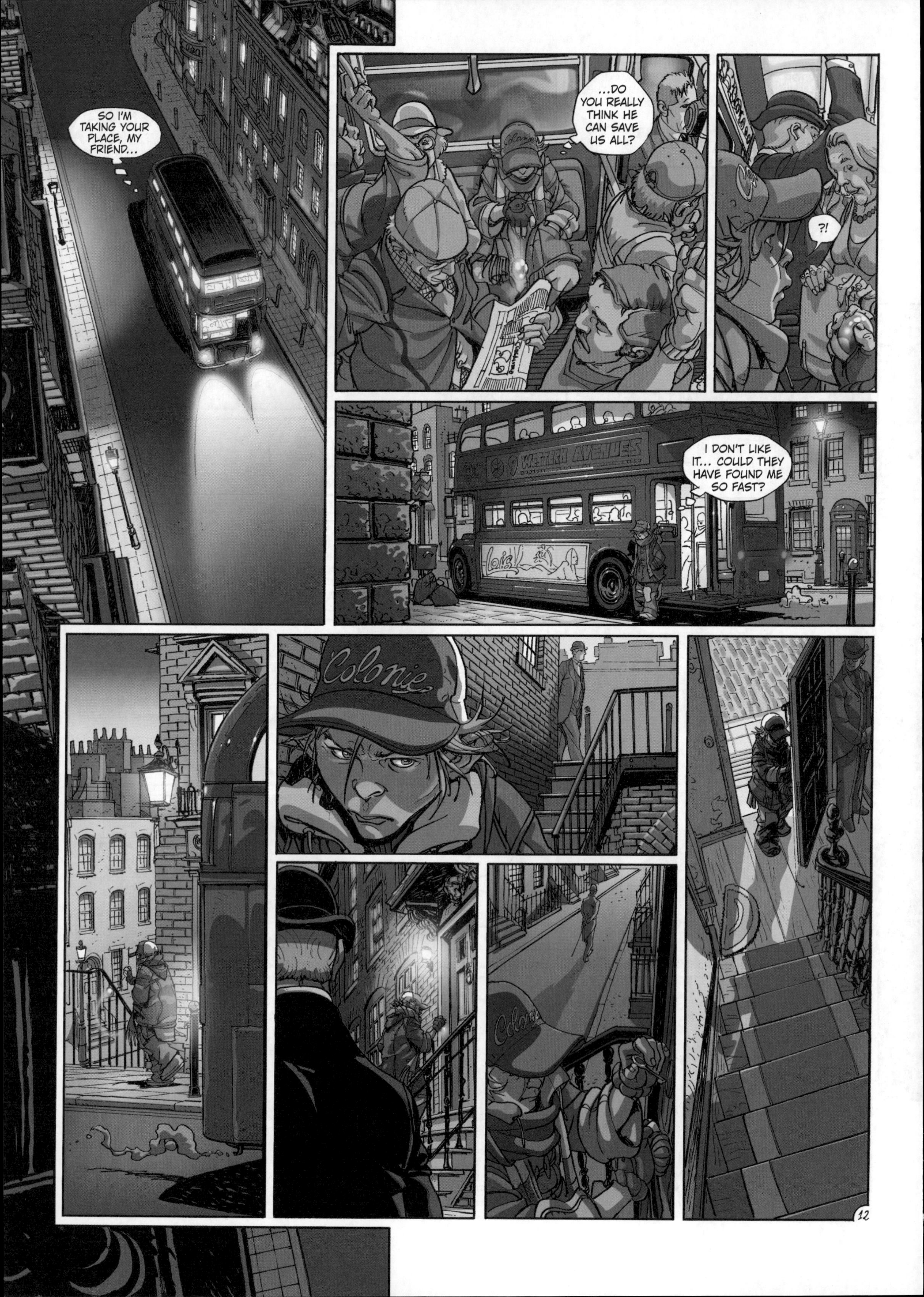
SO I'M TAKING YOUR PLACE, MY FRIEND...
...DO YOU REALLY THINK HE CAN SAVE US ALL?
?!
WESTERN AVENUES
I DON'T LIKE IT... COULD THEY HAVE FOUND ME SO FAST?
Colonie
Colonie

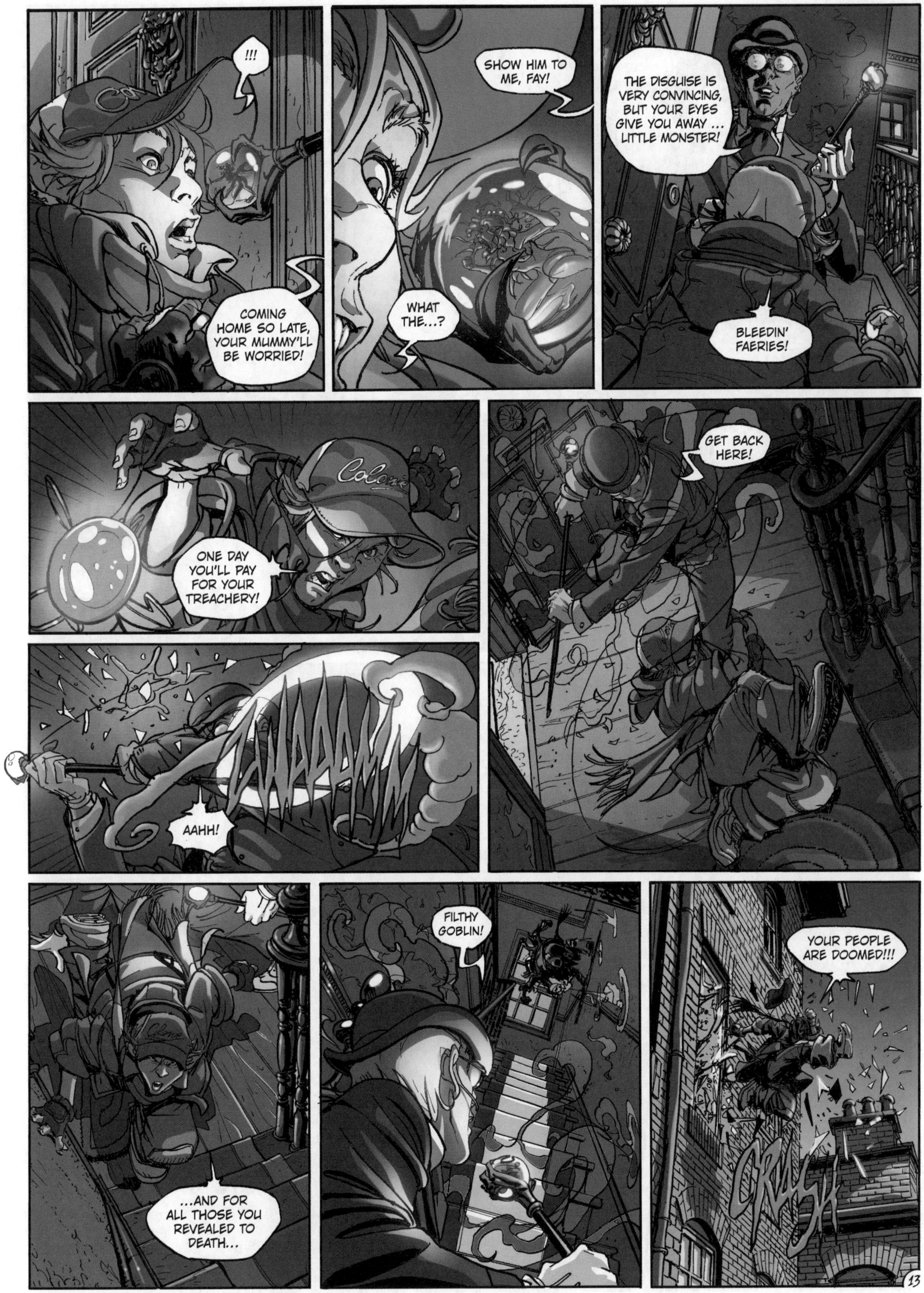
!!!
COMING HOME SO LATE, YOUR MUMMY'LL BE WORRIED!
SHOW HIM TO ME, FAY!
WHAT THE...?
THE DISGUISE IS VERY CONVINCING, BUT YOUR EYES GIVE YOU AWAY ... LITTLE MONSTER!
BLEEDIN' FAERIES!
ONE DAY YOU'LL PAY FOR YOUR TREACHERY!
GET BACK HERE!
AAHH!
...AND FOR ALL THOSE YOU REVEALED TO DEATH...
FILTHY GOBLIN!
YOUR PEOPLE ARE DOOMED!!!
CRASH
13

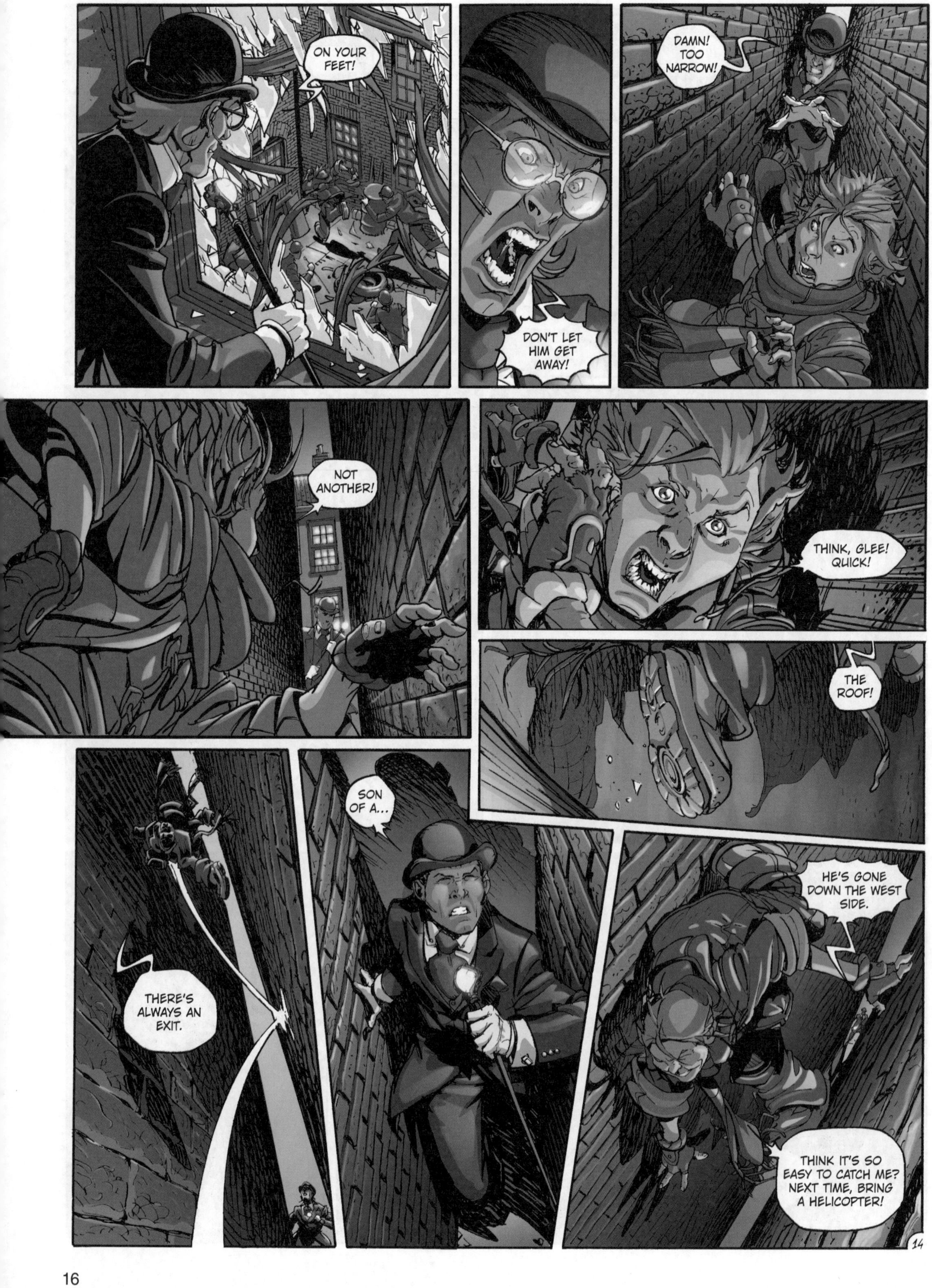
ON YOUR FEET!
DON'T LET HIM GET AWAY!
DAMN! TOO NARROW!
NOT ANOTHER!
THINK, GLEE! QUICK!
THE ROOF!
THERE'S ALWAYS AN EXIT.
SON OF A...
HE'S GONE DOWN THE WEST SIDE.
THINK IT'S SO EASY TO CATCH ME? NEXT TIME, BRING A HELICOPTER!
14

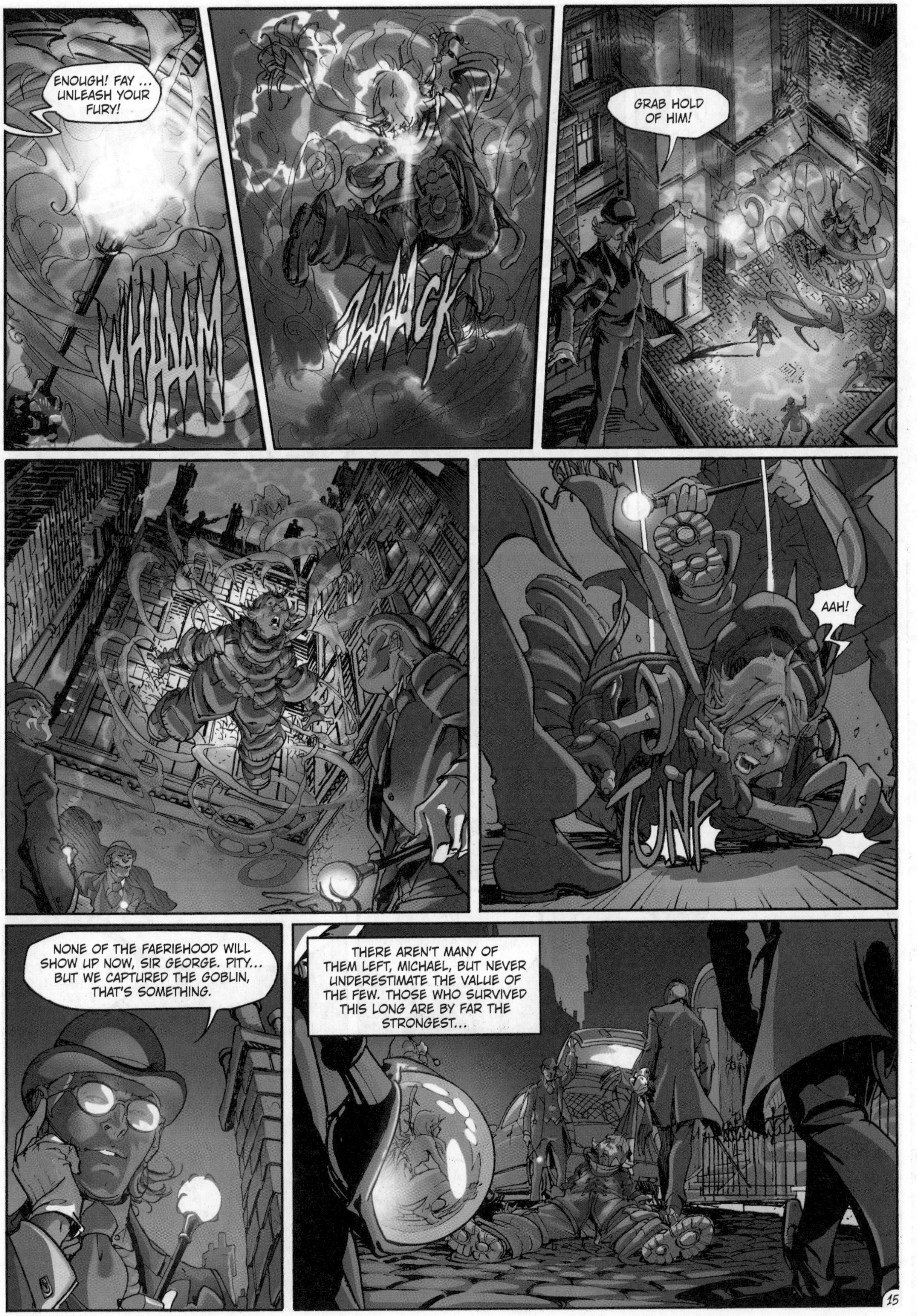
ENOUGH! FAY ... UNLEASH YOUR FURY!
WHAAAM
GRAB HOLD OF HIM!
AAH!
NONE OF THE FAERIEHOOD WILL SHOW UP NOW, SIR GEORGE. PITY... BUT WE CAPTURED THE GOBLIN, THAT'S SOMETHING.
THERE AREN'T MANY OF THEM LEFT, MICHAEL, BUT NEVER UNDERESTIMATE THE VALUE OF THE FEW. THOSE WHO SURVIVED THIS LONG ARE BY FAR THE STRONGEST...

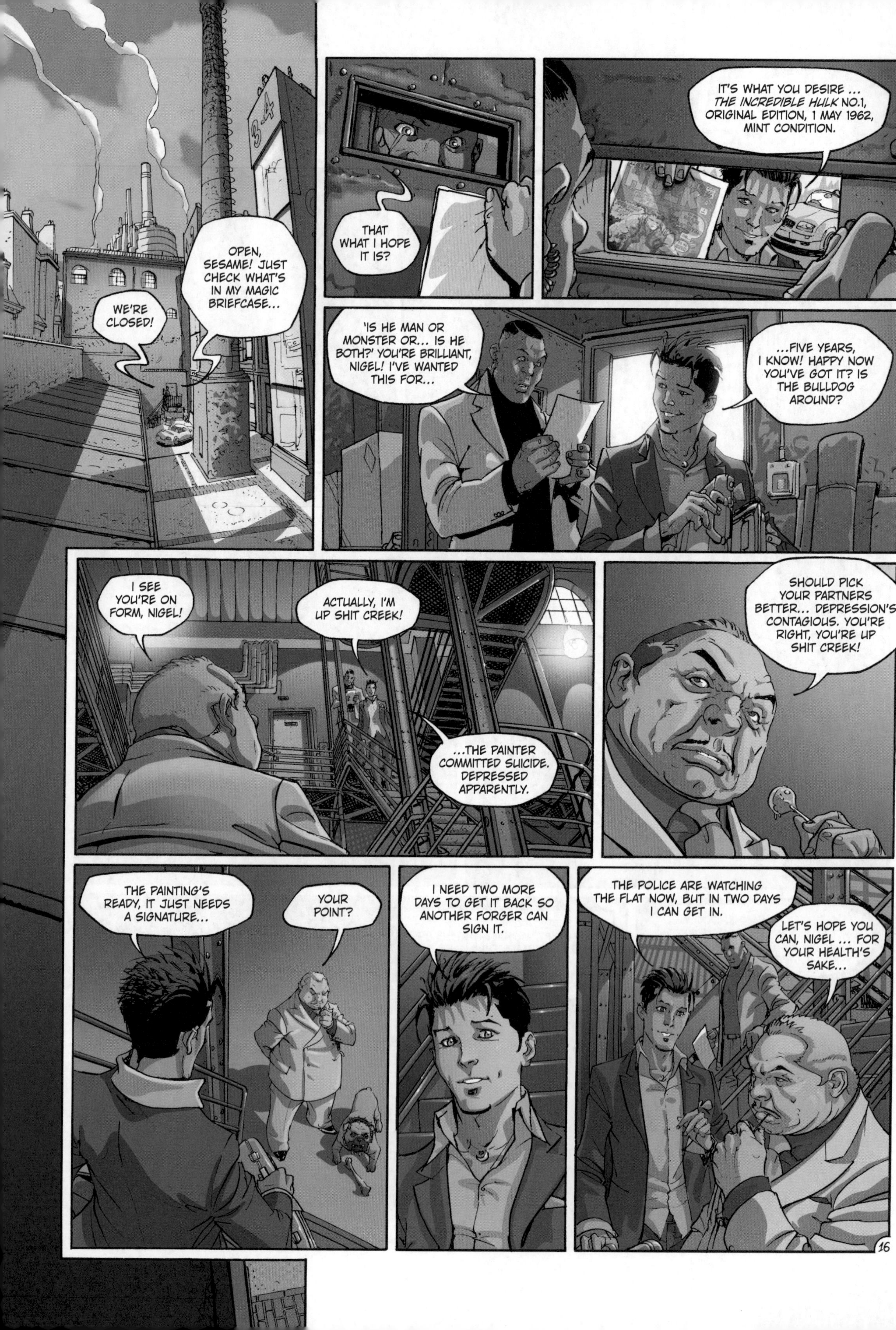
WE'RE CLOSED!
OPEN, SESAME! JUST CHECK WHAT'S IN MY MAGIC BRIEFCASE...
THAT WHAT I HOPE IT IS?
IT'S WHAT YOU DESIRE ... *THE INCREDIBLE HULK* NO.1, ORIGINAL EDITION, 1 MAY 1962, MINT CONDITION.
'IS HE MAN OR MONSTER OR... IS HE BOTH?' YOU'RE BRILLIANT, NIGEL! I'VE WANTED THIS FOR...
...FIVE YEARS, I KNOW! HAPPY NOW YOU'VE GOT IT? IS THE BULLDOG AROUND?
I SEE YOU'RE ON FORM, NIGEL!
ACTUALLY, I'M UP SHIT CREEK!
...THE PAINTER COMMITTED SUICIDE. DEPRESSED APPARENTLY.
SHOULD PICK YOUR PARTNERS BETTER... DEPRESSION'S CONTAGIOUS. YOU'RE RIGHT, YOU'RE UP SHIT CREEK!
THE PAINTING'S READY, IT JUST NEEDS A SIGNATURE...
YOUR POINT?
I NEED TWO MORE DAYS TO GET IT BACK SO ANOTHER FORGER CAN SIGN IT.
THE POLICE ARE WATCHING THE FLAT NOW, BUT IN TWO DAYS I CAN GET IN.
LET'S HOPE YOU CAN, NIGEL ... FOR YOUR HEALTH'S SAKE...

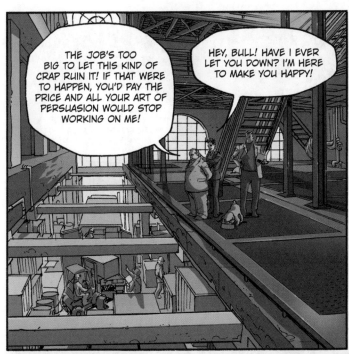

THE JOB'S TOO BIG TO LET THIS KIND OF CRAP RUIN IT! IF THAT WERE TO HAPPEN, YOU'D PAY THE PRICE AND ALL YOUR ART OF PERSUASION WOULD STOP WORKING ON ME!

HEY, BULL! HAVE I EVER LET YOU DOWN? I'M HERE TO MAKE YOU HAPPY!

MITTS OFF, NIGEL...

THE BULLDOG DON'T LIKE BEING STROKED...

RWOF!

SORRY, NIGEL, BUT I'M UNDER STRICT ORDERS.

OK, OK, SESAME... I GET IT. I HARDLY TOUCHED HIM!

LITTLE GIT!

YOU'VE GOT TWO DAYS.

NOW, DEAR MR KARFELD, WHAT'S OUR NETWORK GOT ON YOU?

NEW SCOTLAND YARD

HMM... NOTHING HERE...

NOR HERE... LET'S CHECK THE BANK...

HMM... YOU WERE A GHOST WELL BEFORE YOU PASSED AWAY, JOHN!

19

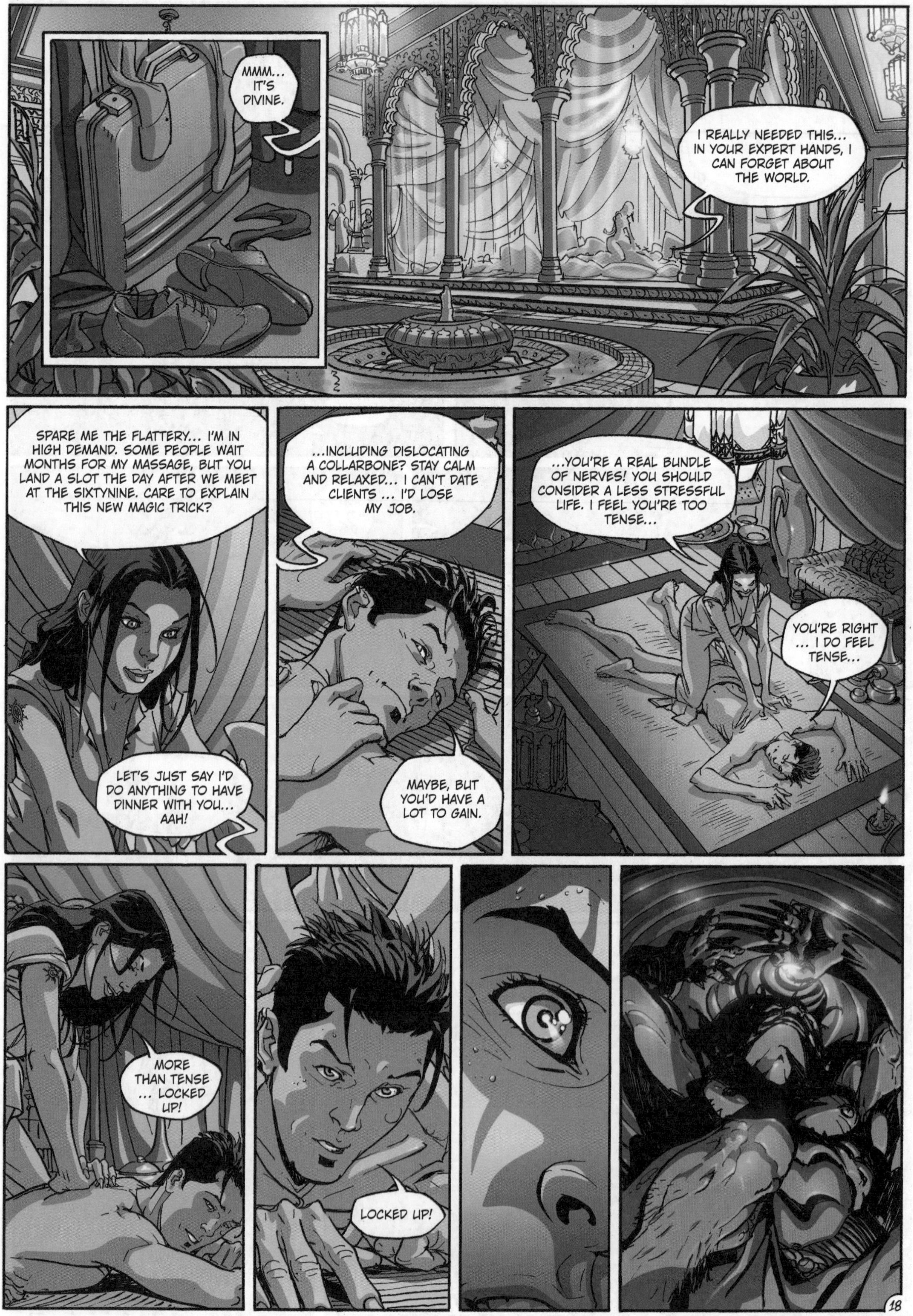
MMM... IT'S DIVINE.
I REALLY NEEDED THIS... IN YOUR EXPERT HANDS, I CAN FORGET ABOUT THE WORLD.
SPARE ME THE FLATTERY... I'M IN HIGH DEMAND. SOME PEOPLE WAIT MONTHS FOR MY MASSAGE, BUT YOU LAND A SLOT THE DAY AFTER WE MEET AT THE SIXTYNINE. CARE TO EXPLAIN THIS NEW MAGIC TRICK?
LET'S JUST SAY I'D DO ANYTHING TO HAVE DINNER WITH YOU... AAH!
...INCLUDING DISLOCATING A COLLARBONE? STAY CALM AND RELAXED... I CAN'T DATE CLIENTS ... I'D LOSE MY JOB.
MAYBE, BUT YOU'D HAVE A LOT TO GAIN.
...YOU'RE A REAL BUNDLE OF NERVES! YOU SHOULD CONSIDER A LESS STRESSFUL LIFE. I FEEL YOU'RE TOO TENSE...
YOU'RE RIGHT ... I DO FEEL TENSE...
MORE THAN TENSE ... LOCKED UP!
LOCKED UP!
18

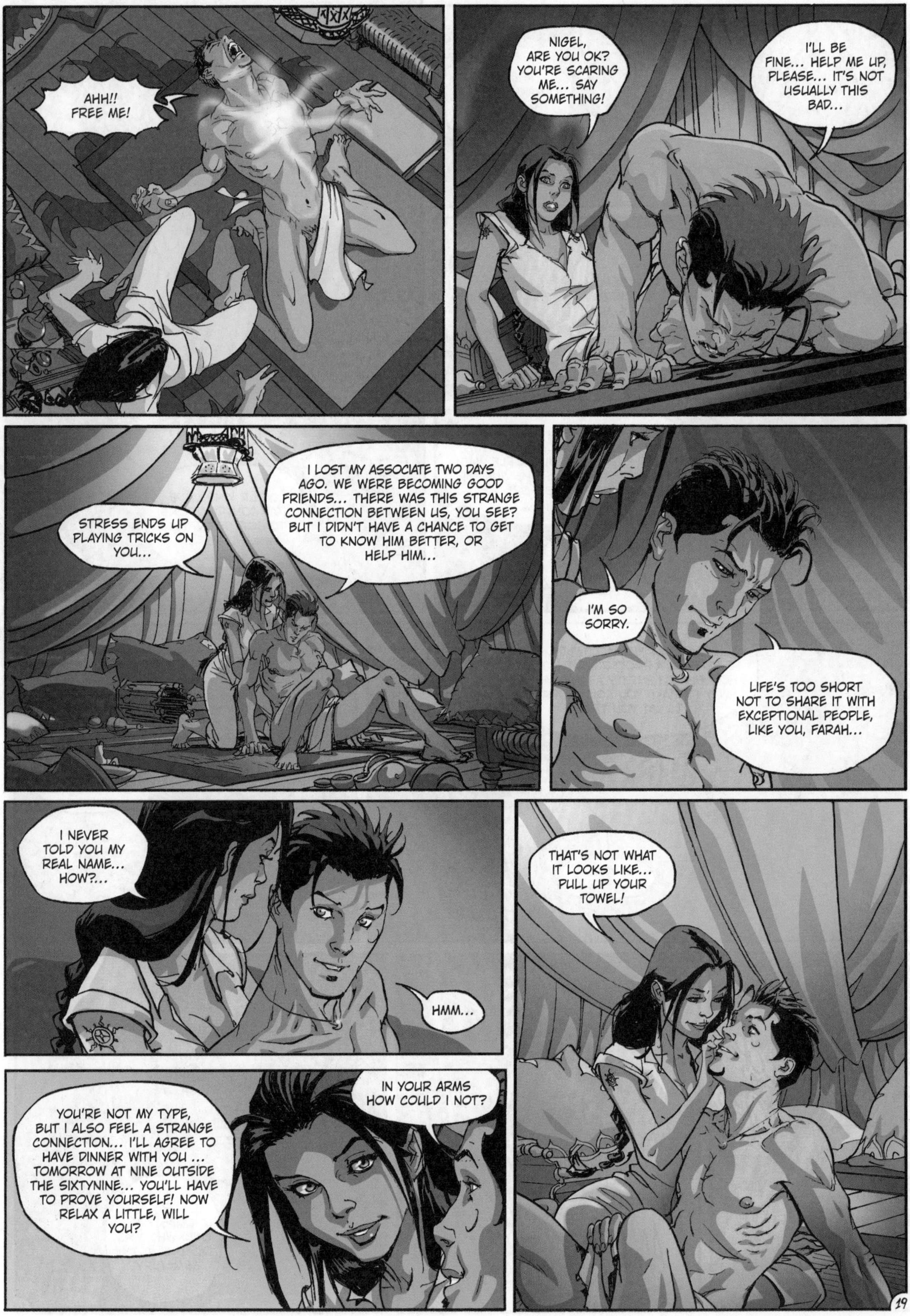
AHH!! FREE ME!
NIGEL, ARE YOU OK? YOU'RE SCARING ME... SAY SOMETHING!
I'LL BE FINE... HELP ME UP, PLEASE... IT'S NOT USUALLY THIS BAD...
STRESS ENDS UP PLAYING TRICKS ON YOU...
I LOST MY ASSOCIATE TWO DAYS AGO. WE WERE BECOMING GOOD FRIENDS... THERE WAS THIS STRANGE CONNECTION BETWEEN US, YOU SEE? BUT I DIDN'T HAVE A CHANCE TO GET TO KNOW HIM BETTER, OR HELP HIM...
I'M SO SORRY.
LIFE'S TOO SHORT NOT TO SHARE IT WITH EXCEPTIONAL PEOPLE, LIKE YOU, FARAH...
I NEVER TOLD YOU MY REAL NAME... HOW?...
HMM...
THAT'S NOT WHAT IT LOOKS LIKE... PULL UP YOUR TOWEL!
YOU'RE NOT MY TYPE, BUT I ALSO FEEL A STRANGE CONNECTION... I'LL AGREE TO HAVE DINNER WITH YOU ... TOMORROW AT NINE OUTSIDE THE SIXTYNINE... YOU'LL HAVE TO PROVE YOURSELF! NOW RELAX A LITTLE, WILL YOU?
IN YOUR ARMS HOW COULD I NOT?
19

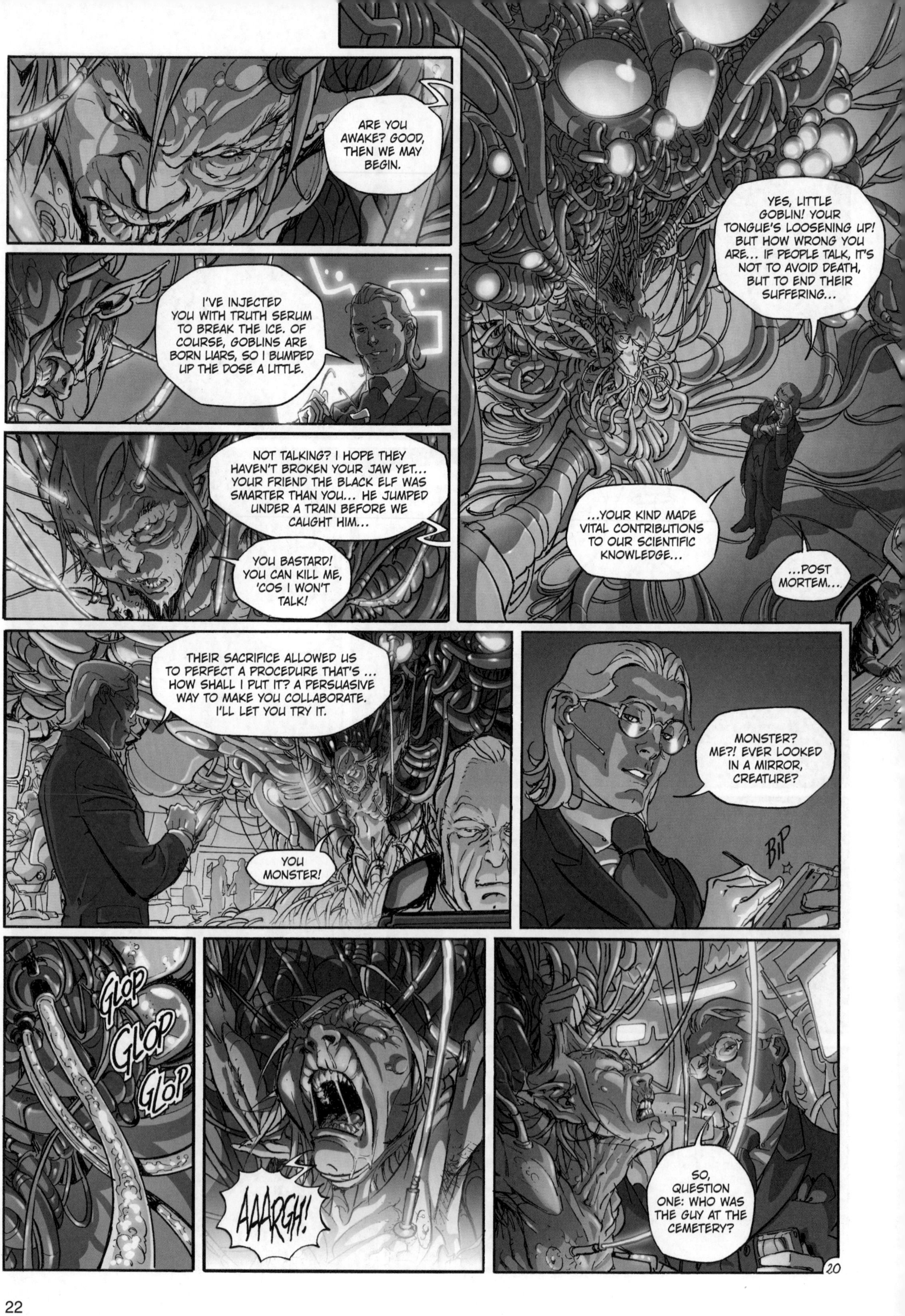
ARE YOU AWAKE? GOOD, THEN WE MAY BEGIN.
I'VE INJECTED YOU WITH TRUTH SERUM TO BREAK THE ICE. OF COURSE, GOBLINS ARE BORN LIARS, SO I BUMPED UP THE DOSE A LITTLE.
NOT TALKING? I HOPE THEY HAVEN'T BROKEN YOUR JAW YET... YOUR FRIEND THE BLACK ELF WAS SMARTER THAN YOU... HE JUMPED UNDER A TRAIN BEFORE WE CAUGHT HIM...
YOU BASTARD! YOU CAN KILL ME, 'COS I WON'T TALK!
YES, LITTLE GOBLIN! YOUR TONGUE'S LOOSENING UP! BUT HOW WRONG YOU ARE... IF PEOPLE TALK, IT'S NOT TO AVOID DEATH, BUT TO END THEIR SUFFERING...
...YOUR KIND MADE VITAL CONTRIBUTIONS TO OUR SCIENTIFIC KNOWLEDGE...
...POST MORTEM...
THEIR SACRIFICE ALLOWED US TO PERFECT A PROCEDURE THAT'S ... HOW SHALL I PUT IT? A PERSUASIVE WAY TO MAKE YOU COLLABORATE. I'LL LET YOU TRY IT.
YOU MONSTER!
MONSTER? ME?! EVER LOOKED IN A MIRROR, CREATURE?
BIP
GLOP
GLOP
GLOP
AAARGH!
SO, QUESTION ONE: WHO WAS THE GUY AT THE CEMETERY?
20

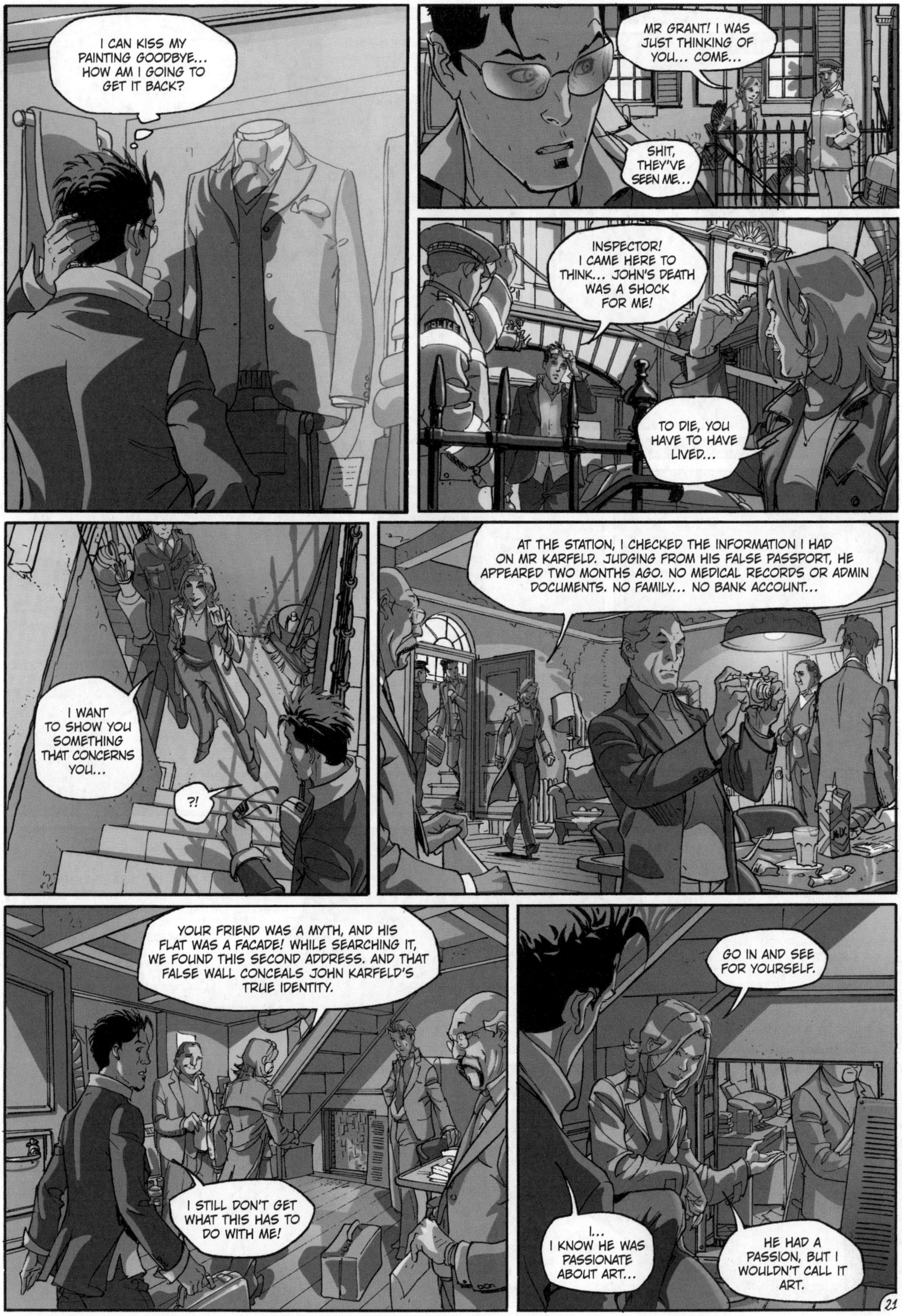

I CAN KISS MY PAINTING GOODBYE... HOW AM I GOING TO GET IT BACK?
MR GRANT! I WAS JUST THINKING OF YOU... COME...
SHIT, THEY'VE SEEN ME...
INSPECTOR! I CAME HERE TO THINK... JOHN'S DEATH WAS A SHOCK FOR ME!
TO DIE, YOU HAVE TO HAVE LIVED...
I WANT TO SHOW YOU SOMETHING THAT CONCERNS YOU...
?!
AT THE STATION, I CHECKED THE INFORMATION I HAD ON MR KARFELD. JUDGING FROM HIS FALSE PASSPORT, HE APPEARED TWO MONTHS AGO. NO MEDICAL RECORDS OR ADMIN DOCUMENTS. NO FAMILY... NO BANK ACCOUNT...
YOUR FRIEND WAS A MYTH, AND HIS FLAT WAS A FACADE! WHILE SEARCHING IT, WE FOUND THIS SECOND ADDRESS. AND THAT FALSE WALL CONCEALS JOHN KARFELD'S TRUE IDENTITY.
I STILL DON'T GET WHAT THIS HAS TO DO WITH ME!
GO IN AND SEE FOR YOURSELF.
I... I KNOW HE WAS PASSIONATE ABOUT ART...
HE HAD A PASSION, BUT I WOULDN'T CALL IT ART.
21

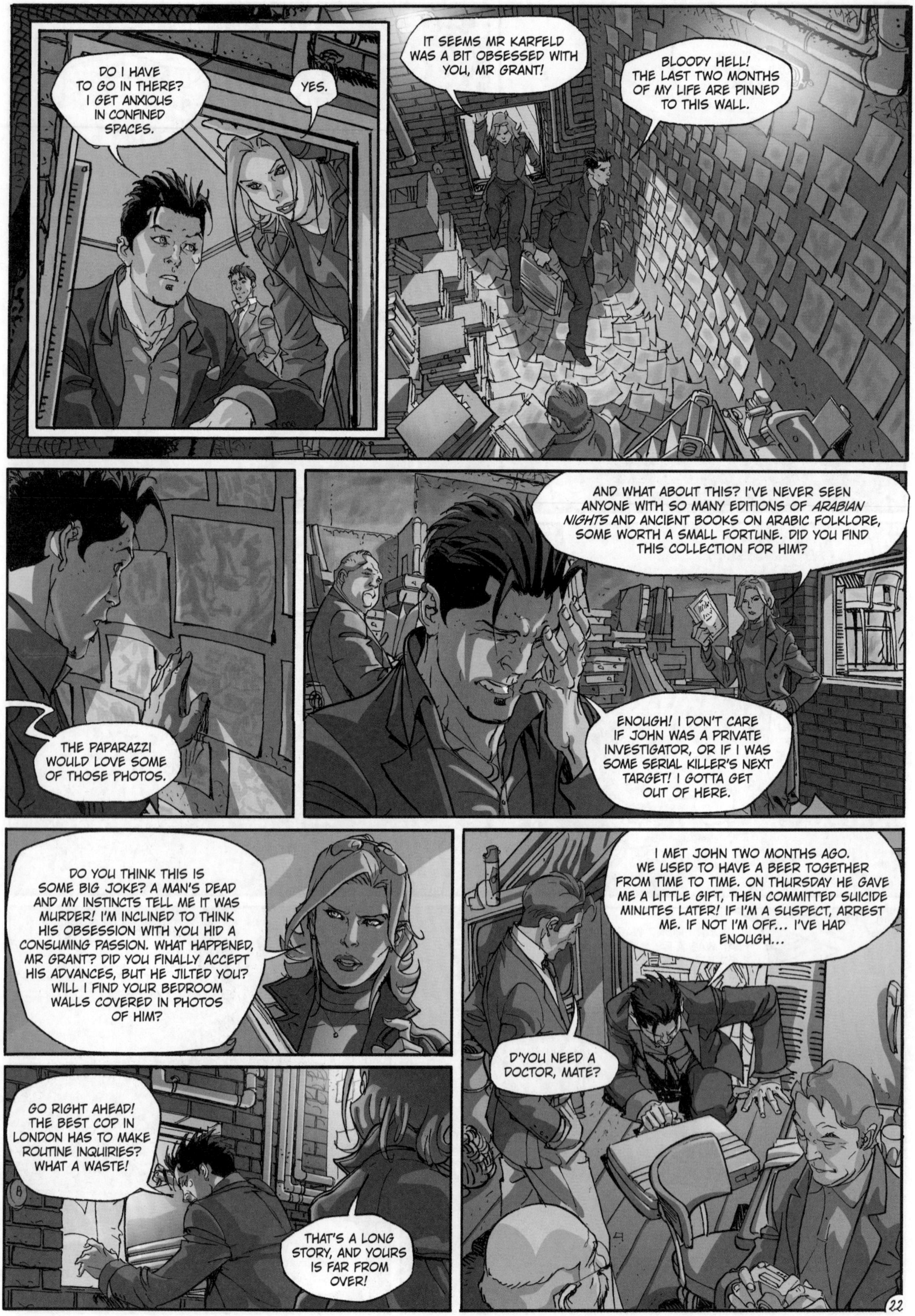
DO I HAVE TO GO IN THERE? I GET ANXIOUS IN CONFINED SPACES.
YES.
IT SEEMS MR KARFELD WAS A BIT OBSESSED WITH YOU, MR GRANT!
BLOODY HELL! THE LAST TWO MONTHS OF MY LIFE ARE PINNED TO THIS WALL.
THE PAPARAZZI WOULD LOVE SOME OF THOSE PHOTOS.
AND WHAT ABOUT THIS? I'VE NEVER SEEN ANYONE WITH SO MANY EDITIONS OF *ARABIAN NIGHTS* AND ANCIENT BOOKS ON ARABIC FOLKLORE, SOME WORTH A SMALL FORTUNE. DID YOU FIND THIS COLLECTION FOR HIM?
ENOUGH! I DON'T CARE IF JOHN WAS A PRIVATE INVESTIGATOR, OR IF I WAS SOME SERIAL KILLER'S NEXT TARGET! I GOTTA GET OUT OF HERE.
DO YOU THINK THIS IS SOME BIG JOKE? A MAN'S DEAD AND MY INSTINCTS TELL ME IT WAS MURDER! I'M INCLINED TO THINK HIS OBSESSION WITH YOU HID A CONSUMING PASSION. WHAT HAPPENED, MR GRANT? DID YOU FINALLY ACCEPT HIS ADVANCES, BUT HE JILTED YOU? WILL I FIND YOUR BEDROOM WALLS COVERED IN PHOTOS OF HIM?
GO RIGHT AHEAD! THE BEST COP IN LONDON HAS TO MAKE ROUTINE INQUIRIES? WHAT A WASTE!
THAT'S A LONG STORY, AND YOURS IS FAR FROM OVER!
I MET JOHN TWO MONTHS AGO. WE USED TO HAVE A BEER TOGETHER FROM TIME TO TIME. ON THURSDAY HE GAVE ME A LITTLE GIFT, THEN COMMITTED SUICIDE MINUTES LATER! IF I'M A SUSPECT, ARREST ME. IF NOT I'M OFF... I'VE HAD ENOUGH...
D'YOU NEED A DOCTOR, MATE?
22

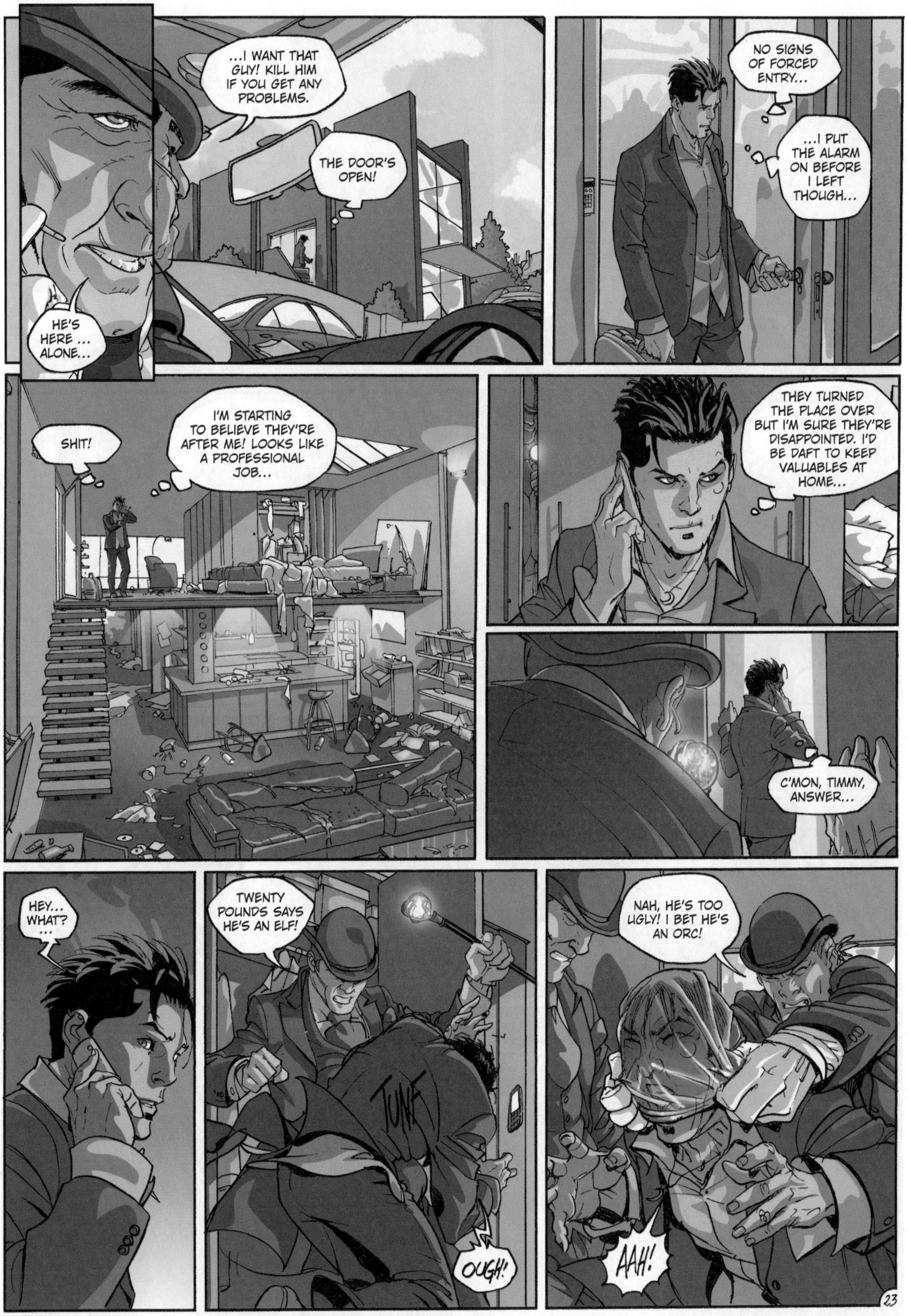
HE'S HERE ... ALONE...
...I WANT THAT GUY! KILL HIM IF YOU GET ANY PROBLEMS.
THE DOOR'S OPEN!
NO SIGNS OF FORCED ENTRY...
...I PUT THE ALARM ON BEFORE I LEFT THOUGH...
SHIT!
I'M STARTING TO BELIEVE THEY'RE AFTER ME! LOOKS LIKE A PROFESSIONAL JOB...
THEY TURNED THE PLACE OVER BUT I'M SURE THEY'RE DISAPPOINTED. I'D BE DAFT TO KEEP VALUABLES AT HOME...
C'MON, TIMMY, ANSWER...
HEY... WHAT? ...
TWENTY POUNDS SAYS HE'S AN ELF!
TUNF
OUGH!
NAH, HE'S TOO UGLY! I BET HE'S AN ORC!
AAH!
23

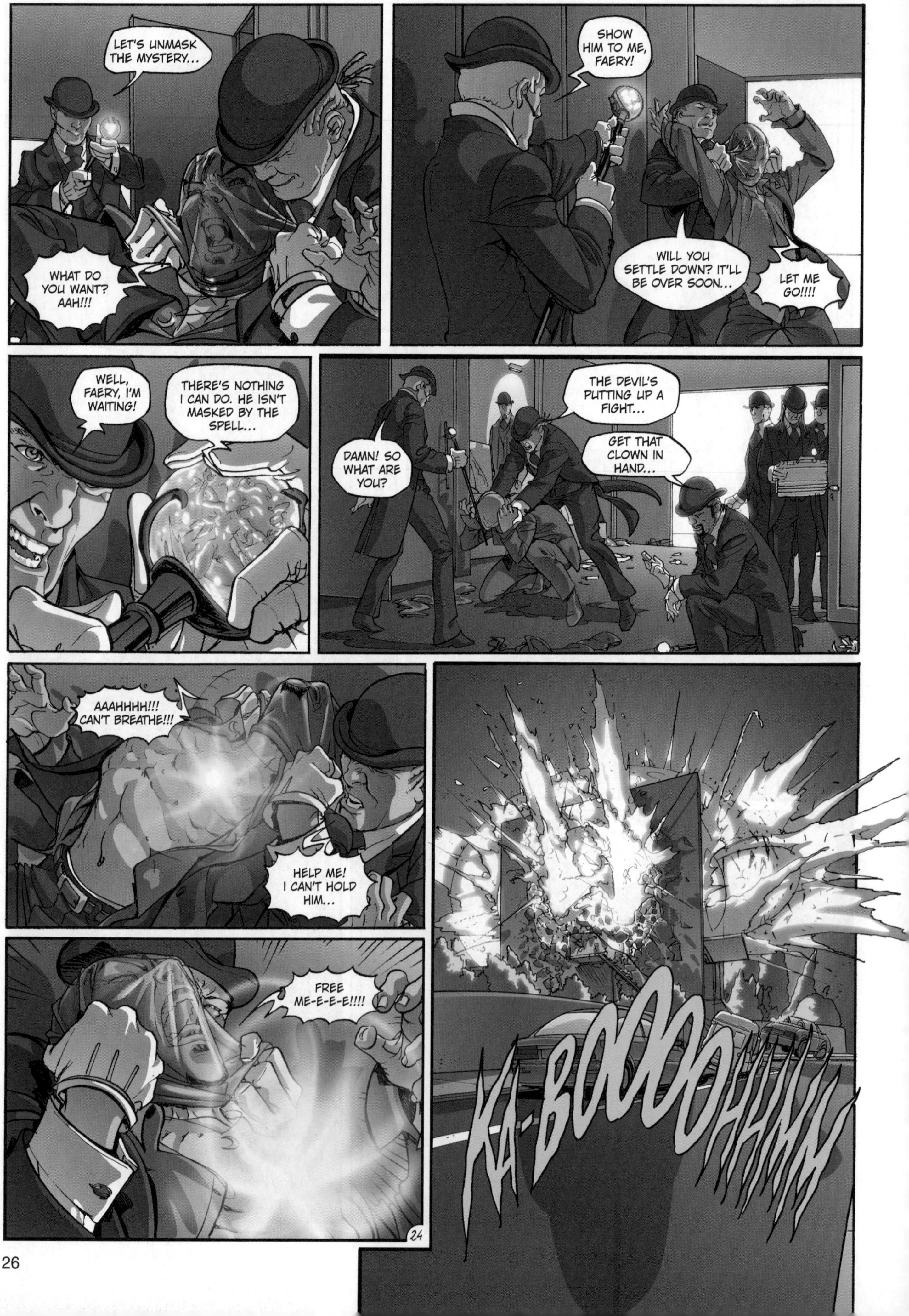
LET'S UNMASK THE MYSTERY...
WHAT DO YOU WANT? AAH!!!
SHOW HIM TO ME, FAERY!
WILL YOU SETTLE DOWN? IT'LL BE OVER SOON...
LET ME GO!!!!
WELL, FAERY, I'M WAITING!
THERE'S NOTHING I CAN DO. HE ISN'T MASKED BY THE SPELL...
THE DEVIL'S PUTTING UP A FIGHT...
DAMN! SO WHAT ARE YOU?
GET THAT CLOWN IN HAND...
AAAHHHH!!! CAN'T BREATHE!!!
HELP ME! I CAN'T HOLD HIM...
FREE ME-E-E-E!!!!
KA-BOOOOHMM
24

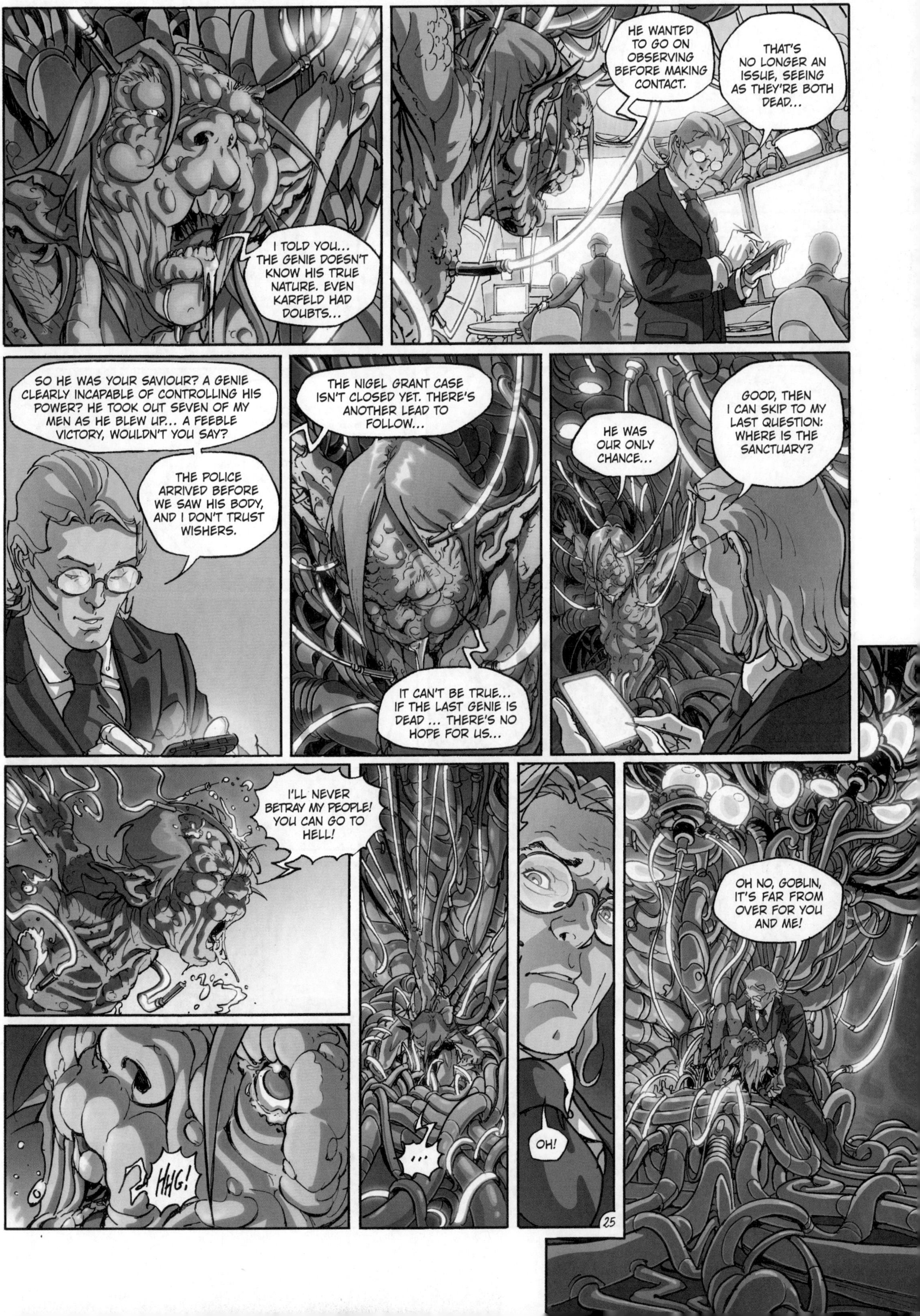
I TOLD YOU... THE GENIE DOESN'T KNOW HIS TRUE NATURE. EVEN KARFELD HAD DOUBTS...
HE WANTED TO GO ON OBSERVING BEFORE MAKING CONTACT.
THAT'S NO LONGER AN ISSUE, SEEING AS THEY'RE BOTH DEAD...
SO HE WAS YOUR SAVIOUR? A GENIE CLEARLY INCAPABLE OF CONTROLLING HIS POWER? HE TOOK OUT SEVEN OF MY MEN AS HE BLEW UP... A FEEBLE VICTORY, WOULDN'T YOU SAY?
THE POLICE ARRIVED BEFORE WE SAW HIS BODY, AND I DON'T TRUST WISHERS.
THE NIGEL GRANT CASE ISN'T CLOSED YET. THERE'S ANOTHER LEAD TO FOLLOW...
IT CAN'T BE TRUE... IF THE LAST GENIE IS DEAD ... THERE'S NO HOPE FOR US...
HE WAS OUR ONLY CHANCE...
GOOD, THEN I CAN SKIP TO MY LAST QUESTION: WHERE IS THE SANCTUARY?
I'LL NEVER BETRAY MY PEOPLE! YOU CAN GO TO HELL!
HHG!
...
OH!
OH NO, GOBLIN, IT'S FAR FROM OVER FOR YOU AND ME!

WHILE WE FEAR THIS WAS ANOTHER NIGHTMARE TERRORIST ATTACK, THE SECRET SERVICES HAVE JUST ANNOUNCED THAT THE TRAGIC BLAST THAT OCCURRED LESS THAN AN HOUR AGO WAS SIMPLY A DOMESTIC ACCIDENT...

THE BLAST, DESCRIBED BY WITNESSES AS INTENSELY VIOLENT, BLEW UP THE HOME OF NIGEL GRANT, INJURING SEVERAL PEOPLE IN THE STREETS...

MR GRANT, A SEEMINGLY ORDINARY YOUNG LONDONER, HAD STARTED TO GAIN A SOLID REPUTATION IN THE WORLD OF MODERN ART COLLECTORS AND RARE OBJECT AUCTIONS.

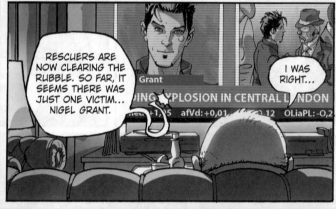

A POLICE SOURCE HAS REVEALED THAT MR GRANT WAS QUESTIONED ABOUT A MAN'S SUICIDE IN PICCADILLY TUBE STATION THREE DAYS AGO. 'JOHN KARFELD', WHOSE REAL IDENTITY REMAINS UNKNOWN, SEEMS TO HAVE ARGUED WITH MR GRANT BEFORE THROWING HIMSELF ONTO THE TRACK.

DID THE TWO MEN HAVE A PROFESSIONAL OR INDEED A ROMANTIC RELATIONSHIP GONE SOUR? WE ARE UNABLE TO SAY AT THIS TIME. INSPECTOR JANE GREY, IN CHARGE OF THE INQUIRY, NEITHER CONFIRMS NOR DENIES IT.

Scotland Yard Inspector

BUILDING EXPLOSION IN CENTRAL LONDON

RESCUERS ARE NOW CLEARING THE RUBBLE. SO FAR, IT SEEMS THERE WAS JUST ONE VICTIM... NIGEL GRANT.

I WAS RIGHT...

Grant

...DING EXPLOSION IN L NDON

...I KNEW THAT LITTLE PILLOCK WAS GAY!

WE'RE GONNA HAVE TO FIND THE DAMN PAINTING ON OUR OWN...

26

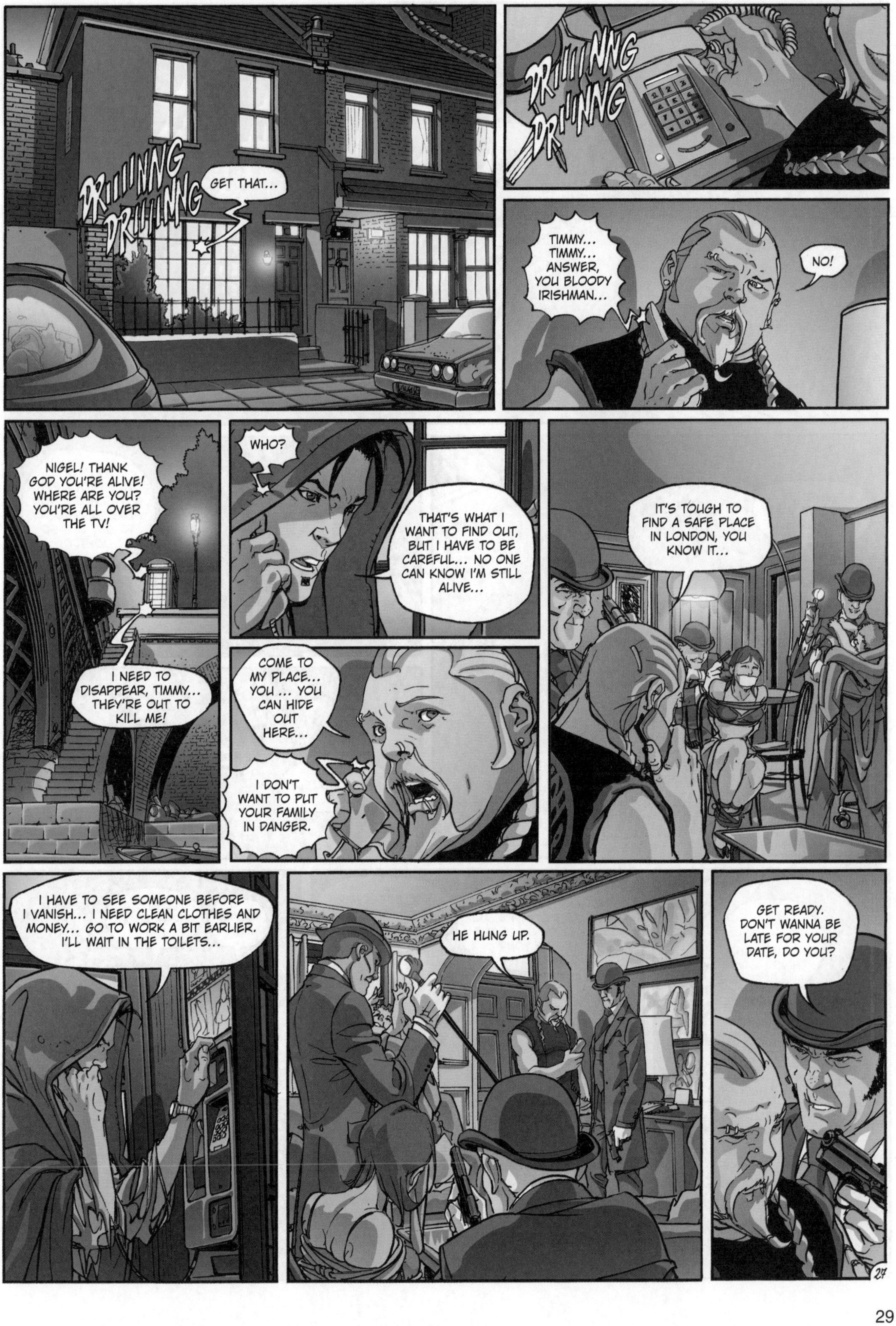
DRIIIINNG DRIIIINNG
GET THAT...
DRIIIINNG DRIIINNG
TIMMY... TIMMY... ANSWER, YOU BLOODY IRISHMAN...
NO!
NIGEL! THANK GOD YOU'RE ALIVE! WHERE ARE YOU? YOU'RE ALL OVER THE TV!
I NEED TO DISAPPEAR, TIMMY... THEY'RE OUT TO KILL ME!
WHO?
THAT'S WHAT I WANT TO FIND OUT, BUT I HAVE TO BE CAREFUL... NO ONE CAN KNOW I'M STILL ALIVE...
COME TO MY PLACE... YOU ... YOU CAN HIDE OUT HERE...
I DON'T WANT TO PUT YOUR FAMILY IN DANGER.
IT'S TOUGH TO FIND A SAFE PLACE IN LONDON, YOU KNOW IT...
I HAVE TO SEE SOMEONE BEFORE I VANISH... I NEED CLEAN CLOTHES AND MONEY... GO TO WORK A BIT EARLIER. I'LL WAIT IN THE TOILETS...
HE HUNG UP.
GET READY. DON'T WANNA BE LATE FOR YOUR DATE, DO YOU?
27

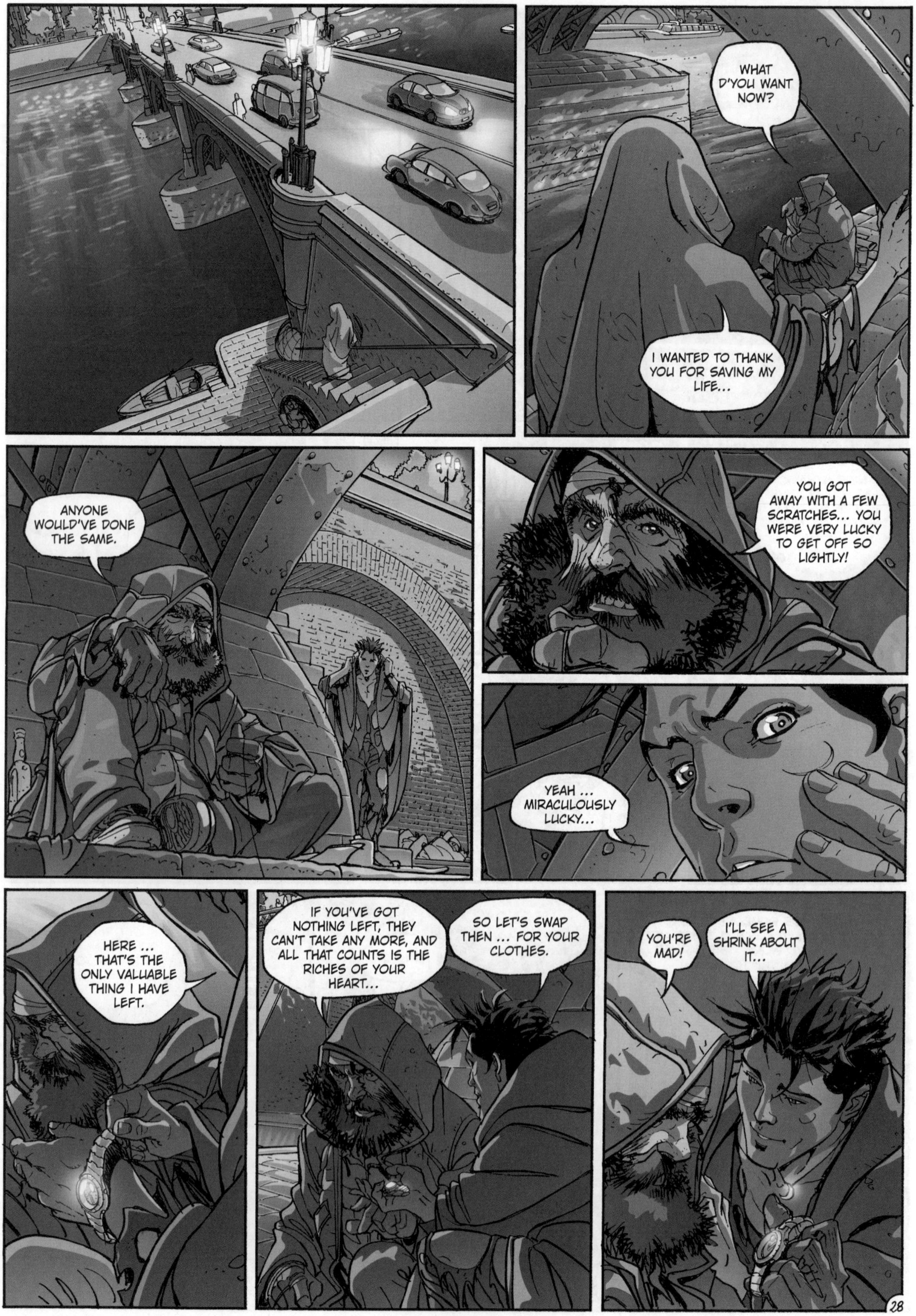
WHAT D'YOU WANT NOW?
I WANTED TO THANK YOU FOR SAVING MY LIFE...
ANYONE WOULD'VE DONE THE SAME.
YOU GOT AWAY WITH A FEW SCRATCHES... YOU WERE VERY LUCKY TO GET OFF SO LIGHTLY!
YEAH ... MIRACULOUSLY LUCKY...
HERE ... THAT'S THE ONLY VALUABLE THING I HAVE LEFT.
IF YOU'VE GOT NOTHING LEFT, THEY CAN'T TAKE ANY MORE, AND ALL THAT COUNTS IS THE RICHES OF YOUR HEART...
SO LET'S SWAP THEN ... FOR YOUR CLOTHES.
YOU'RE MAD!
I'LL SEE A SHRINK ABOUT IT...
28

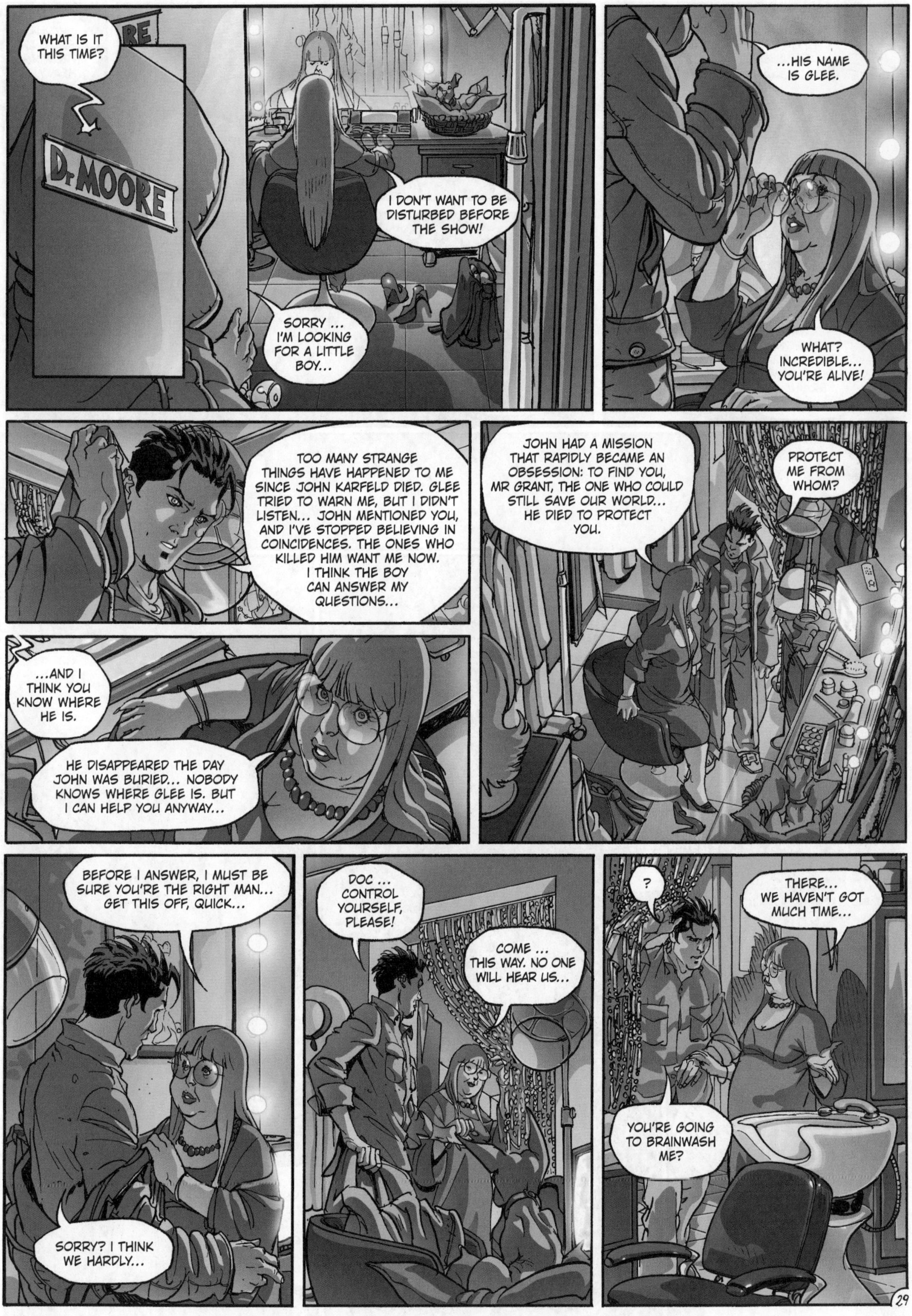
WHAT IS IT THIS TIME?
Dr MOORE
I DON'T WANT TO BE DISTURBED BEFORE THE SHOW!
SORRY ... I'M LOOKING FOR A LITTLE BOY...
...HIS NAME IS GLEE.
WHAT? INCREDIBLE... YOU'RE ALIVE!
TOO MANY STRANGE THINGS HAVE HAPPENED TO ME SINCE JOHN KARFELD DIED. GLEE TRIED TO WARN ME, BUT I DIDN'T LISTEN... JOHN MENTIONED YOU, AND I'VE STOPPED BELIEVING IN COINCIDENCES. THE ONES WHO KILLED HIM WANT ME NOW. I THINK THE BOY CAN ANSWER MY QUESTIONS...
...AND I THINK YOU KNOW WHERE HE IS.
HE DISAPPEARED THE DAY JOHN WAS BURIED... NOBODY KNOWS WHERE GLEE IS. BUT I CAN HELP YOU ANYWAY...
JOHN HAD A MISSION THAT RAPIDLY BECAME AN OBSESSION: TO FIND YOU, MR GRANT, THE ONE WHO COULD STILL SAVE OUR WORLD... HE DIED TO PROTECT YOU.
PROTECT ME FROM WHOM?
BEFORE I ANSWER, I MUST BE SURE YOU'RE THE RIGHT MAN... GET THIS OFF, QUICK...
SORRY? I THINK WE HARDLY...
DOC ... CONTROL YOURSELF, PLEASE!
COME ... THIS WAY. NO ONE WILL HEAR US...
?
THERE... WE HAVEN'T GOT MUCH TIME...
YOU'RE GOING TO BRAINWASH ME?
29

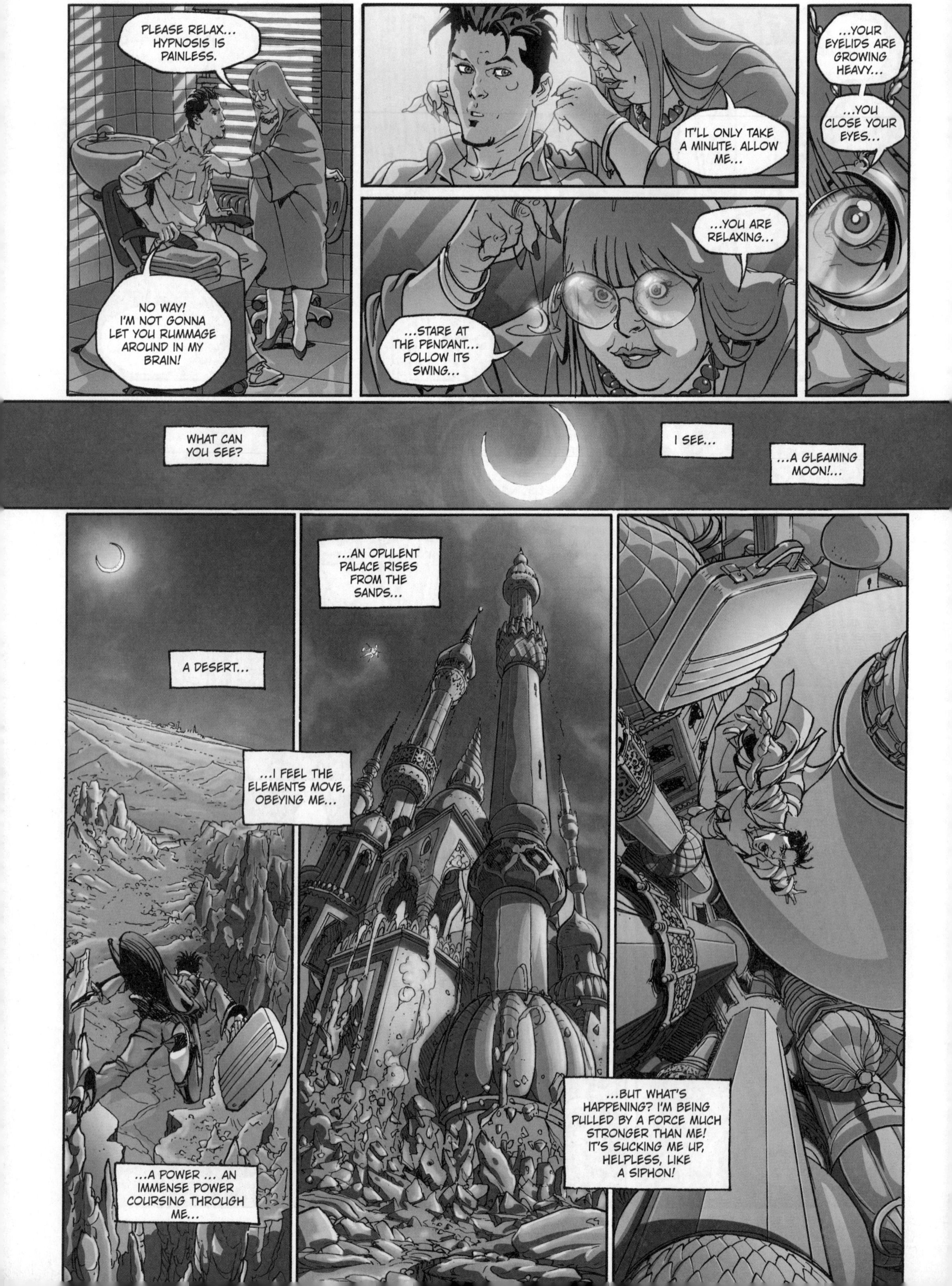
PLEASE RELAX... HYPNOSIS IS PAINLESS.
NO WAY! I'M NOT GONNA LET YOU RUMMAGE AROUND IN MY BRAIN!
IT'LL ONLY TAKE A MINUTE. ALLOW ME...
...STARE AT THE PENDANT... FOLLOW ITS SWING...
...YOU ARE RELAXING...
...YOUR EYELIDS ARE GROWING HEAVY...
...YOU CLOSE YOUR EYES...
WHAT CAN YOU SEE?
I SEE...
...A GLEAMING MOON!...
A DESERT...
...A POWER ... AN IMMENSE POWER COURSING THROUGH ME...
...I FEEL THE ELEMENTS MOVE, OBEYING ME...
...AN OPULENT PALACE RISES FROM THE SANDS...
...BUT WHAT'S HAPPENING? I'M BEING PULLED BY A FORCE MUCH STRONGER THAN ME! IT'S SUCKING ME UP, HELPLESS, LIKE A SIPHON!

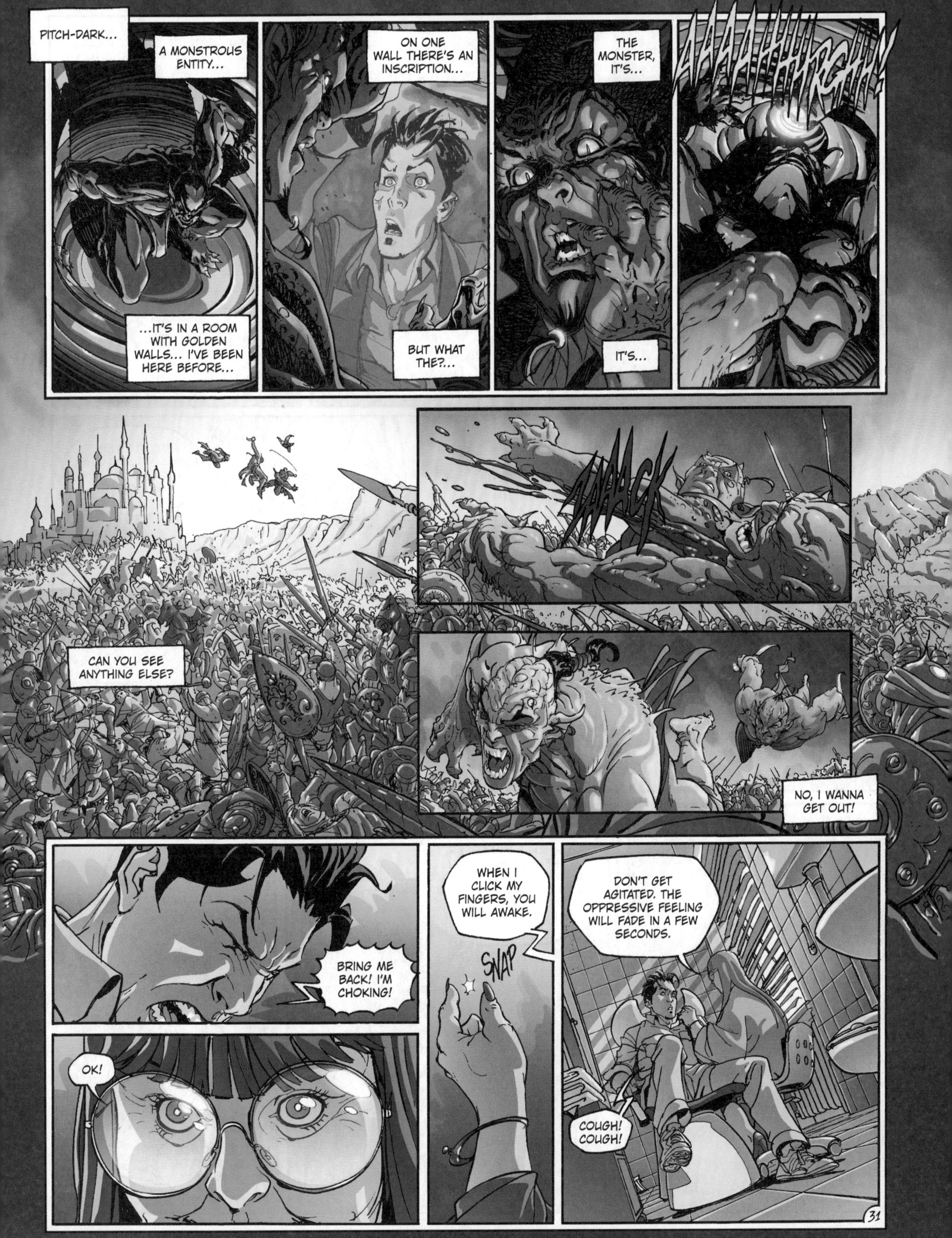
PITCH-DARK...
A MONSTROUS ENTITY...
...IT'S IN A ROOM WITH GOLDEN WALLS... I'VE BEEN HERE BEFORE...
ON ONE WALL THERE'S AN INSCRIPTION...
BUT WHAT THE?...
THE MONSTER, IT'S...
IT'S...
AAAAHHHRGHH!
CAN YOU SEE ANYTHING ELSE?
NO, I WANNA GET OUT!
BRING ME BACK! I'M CHOKING!
OK!
WHEN I CLICK MY FINGERS, YOU WILL AWAKE.
SNAP
DON'T GET AGITATED. THE OPPRESSIVE FEELING WILL FADE IN A FEW SECONDS.
COUGH! COUGH!

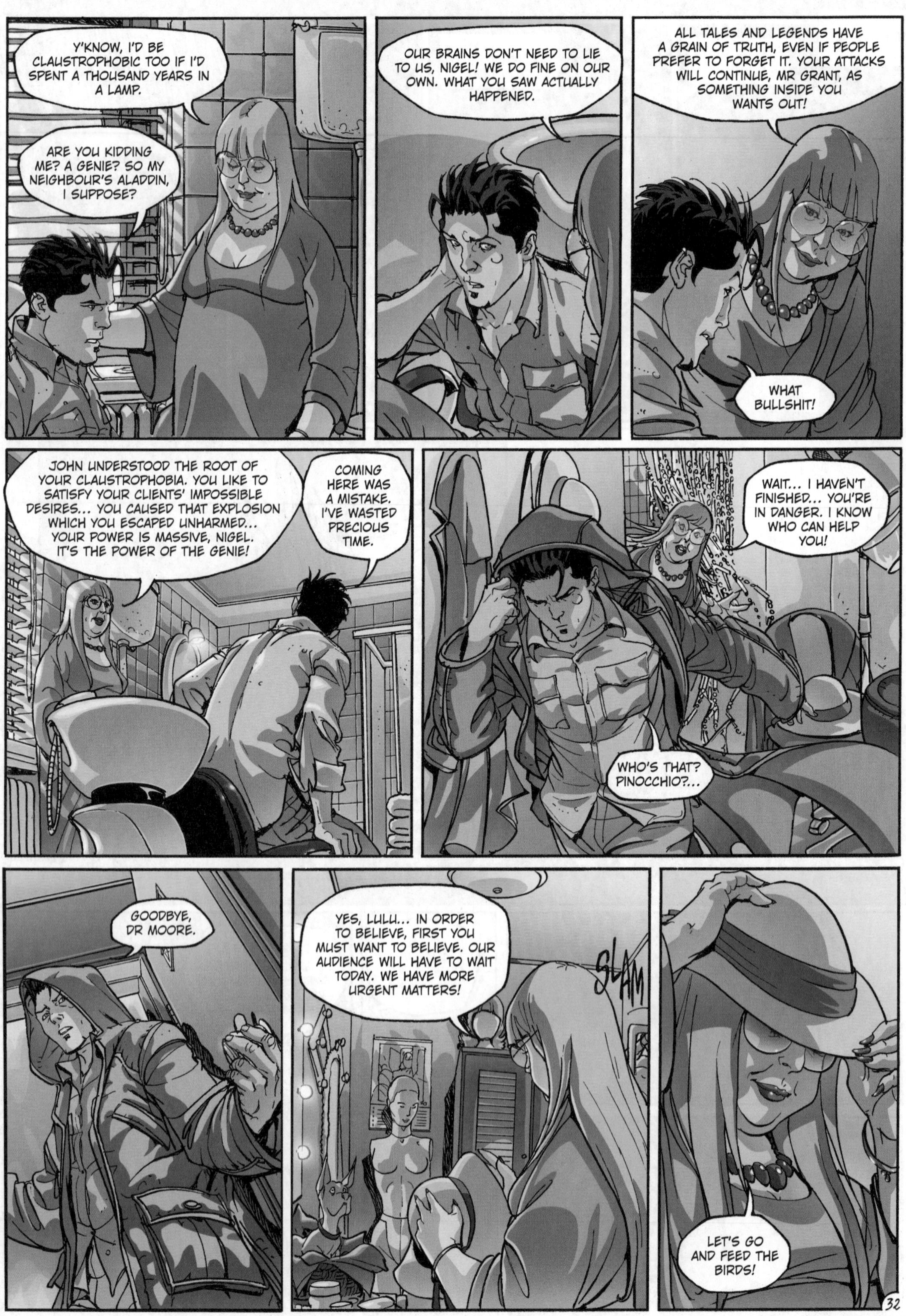

Y'KNOW, I'D BE CLAUSTROPHOBIC TOO IF I'D SPENT A THOUSAND YEARS IN A LAMP.
ARE YOU KIDDING ME? A GENIE? SO MY NEIGHBOUR'S ALADDIN, I SUPPOSE?
OUR BRAINS DON'T NEED TO LIE TO US, NIGEL! WE DO FINE ON OUR OWN. WHAT YOU SAW ACTUALLY HAPPENED.
ALL TALES AND LEGENDS HAVE A GRAIN OF TRUTH, EVEN IF PEOPLE PREFER TO FORGET IT. YOUR ATTACKS WILL CONTINUE, MR GRANT, AS SOMETHING INSIDE YOU WANTS OUT!
WHAT BULLSHIT!
JOHN UNDERSTOOD THE ROOT OF YOUR CLAUSTROPHOBIA. YOU LIKE TO SATISFY YOUR CLIENTS' IMPOSSIBLE DESIRES... YOU CAUSED THAT EXPLOSION WHICH YOU ESCAPED UNHARMED... YOUR POWER IS MASSIVE, NIGEL. IT'S THE POWER OF THE GENIE!
COMING HERE WAS A MISTAKE. I'VE WASTED PRECIOUS TIME.
WAIT... I HAVEN'T FINISHED... YOU'RE IN DANGER. I KNOW WHO CAN HELP YOU!
WHO'S THAT? PINOCCHIO?...
GOODBYE, DR MOORE.
YES, LULU... IN ORDER TO BELIEVE, FIRST YOU MUST WANT TO BELIEVE. OUR AUDIENCE WILL HAVE TO WAIT TODAY. WE HAVE MORE URGENT MATTERS!
SLAM
LET'S GO AND FEED THE BIRDS!
32

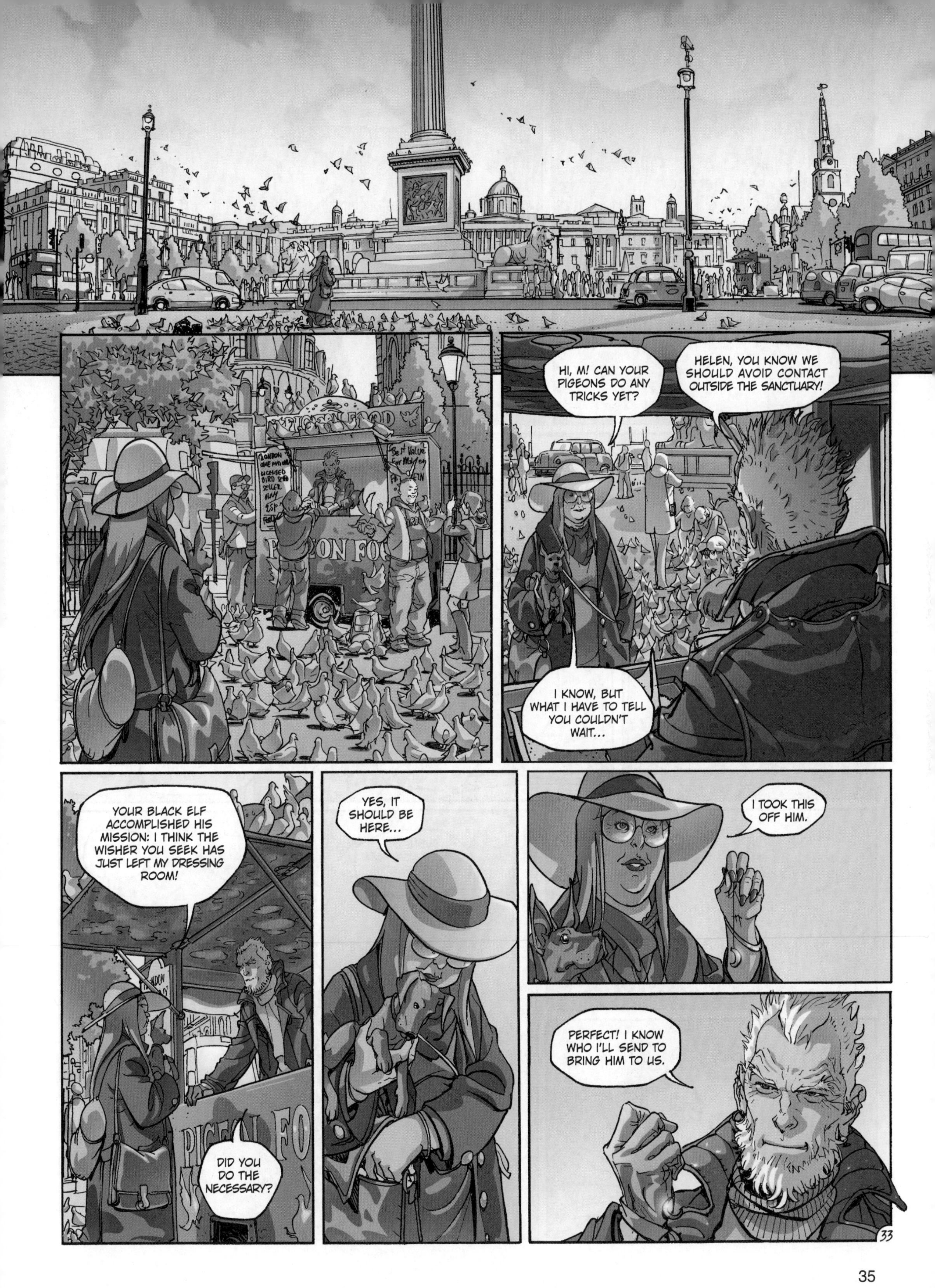
HI, M! CAN YOUR PIGEONS DO ANY TRICKS YET?
HELEN, YOU KNOW WE SHOULD AVOID CONTACT OUTSIDE THE SANCTUARY!
I KNOW, BUT WHAT I HAVE TO TELL YOU COULDN'T WAIT...
YOUR BLACK ELF ACCOMPLISHED HIS MISSION: I THINK THE WISHER YOU SEEK HAS JUST LEFT MY DRESSING ROOM!
DID YOU DO THE NECESSARY?
YES, IT SHOULD BE HERE...
I TOOK THIS OFF HIM.
PERFECT! I KNOW WHO I'LL SEND TO BRING HIM TO US.
33

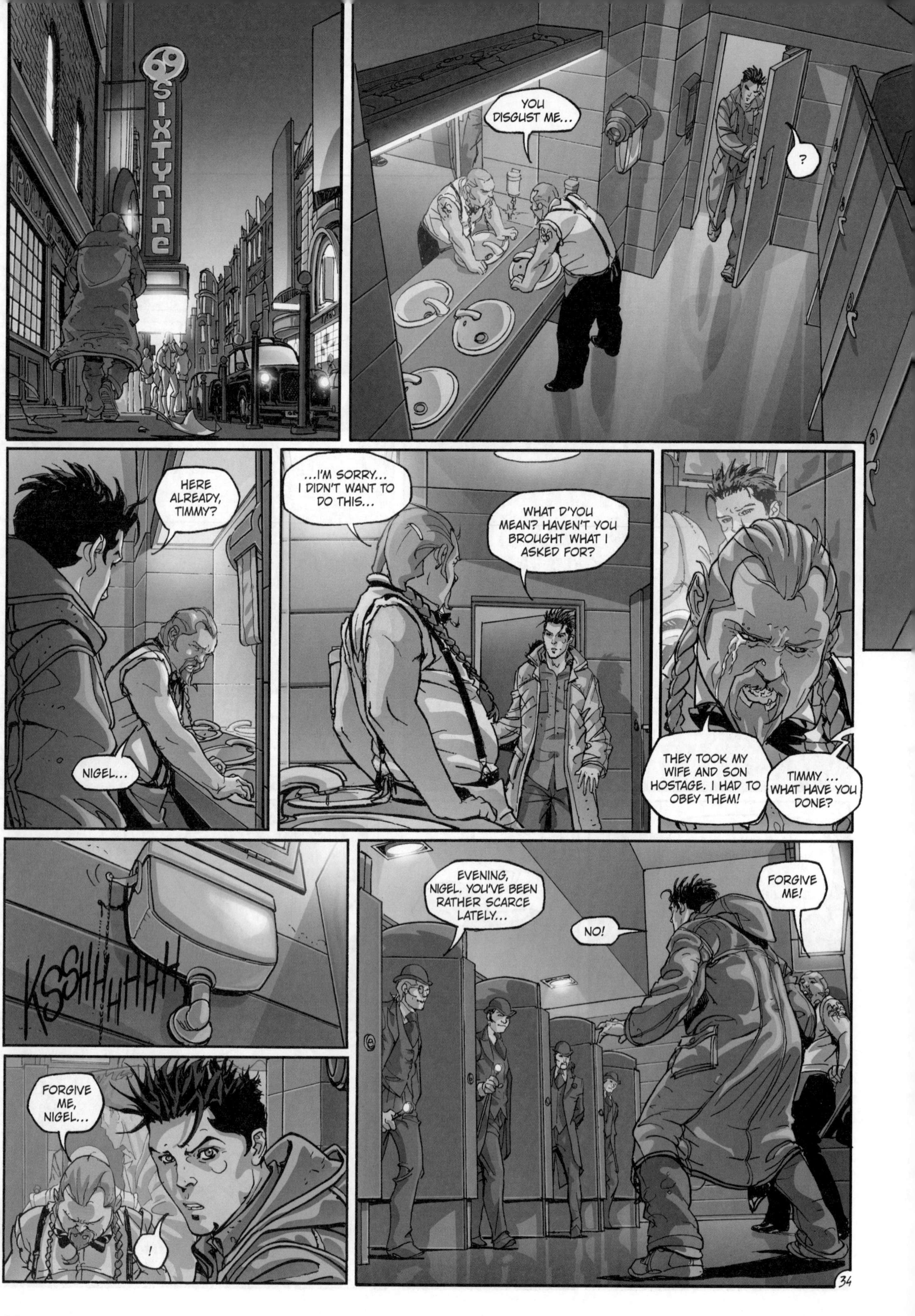
SIXTYNINE
YOU DISGUST ME...
?
HERE ALREADY, TIMMY?
NIGEL...
...I'M SORRY... I DIDN'T WANT TO DO THIS...
WHAT D'YOU MEAN? HAVEN'T YOU BROUGHT WHAT I ASKED FOR?
THEY TOOK MY WIFE AND SON HOSTAGE. I HAD TO OBEY THEM!
TIMMY ... WHAT HAVE YOU DONE?
KSSHHHHHH
FORGIVE ME, NIGEL...
!
EVENING, NIGEL. YOU'VE BEEN RATHER SCARCE LATELY...
NO!
FORGIVE ME!
34

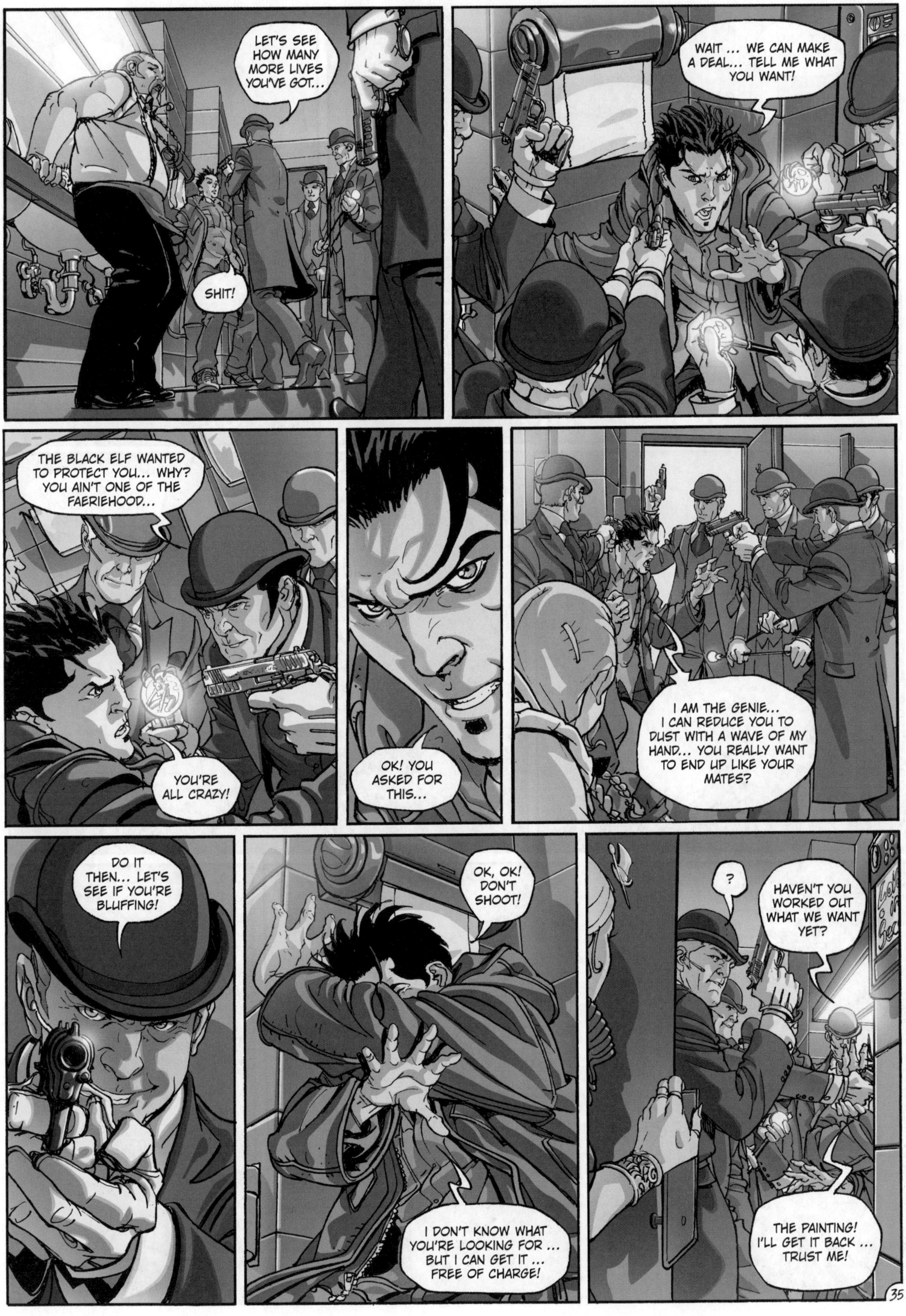
LET'S SEE HOW MANY MORE LIVES YOU'VE GOT...
SHIT!
WAIT ... WE CAN MAKE A DEAL... TELL ME WHAT YOU WANT!
THE BLACK ELF WANTED TO PROTECT YOU... WHY? YOU AIN'T ONE OF THE FAERIEHOOD...
YOU'RE ALL CRAZY!
OK! YOU ASKED FOR THIS...
I AM THE GENIE... I CAN REDUCE YOU TO DUST WITH A WAVE OF MY HAND... YOU REALLY WANT TO END UP LIKE YOUR MATES?
DO IT THEN... LET'S SEE IF YOU'RE BLUFFING!
OK, OK! DON'T SHOOT!
I DON'T KNOW WHAT YOU'RE LOOKING FOR ... BUT I CAN GET IT ... FREE OF CHARGE!
?
HAVEN'T YOU WORKED OUT WHAT WE WANT YET?
THE PAINTING! I'LL GET IT BACK ... TRUST ME!
35

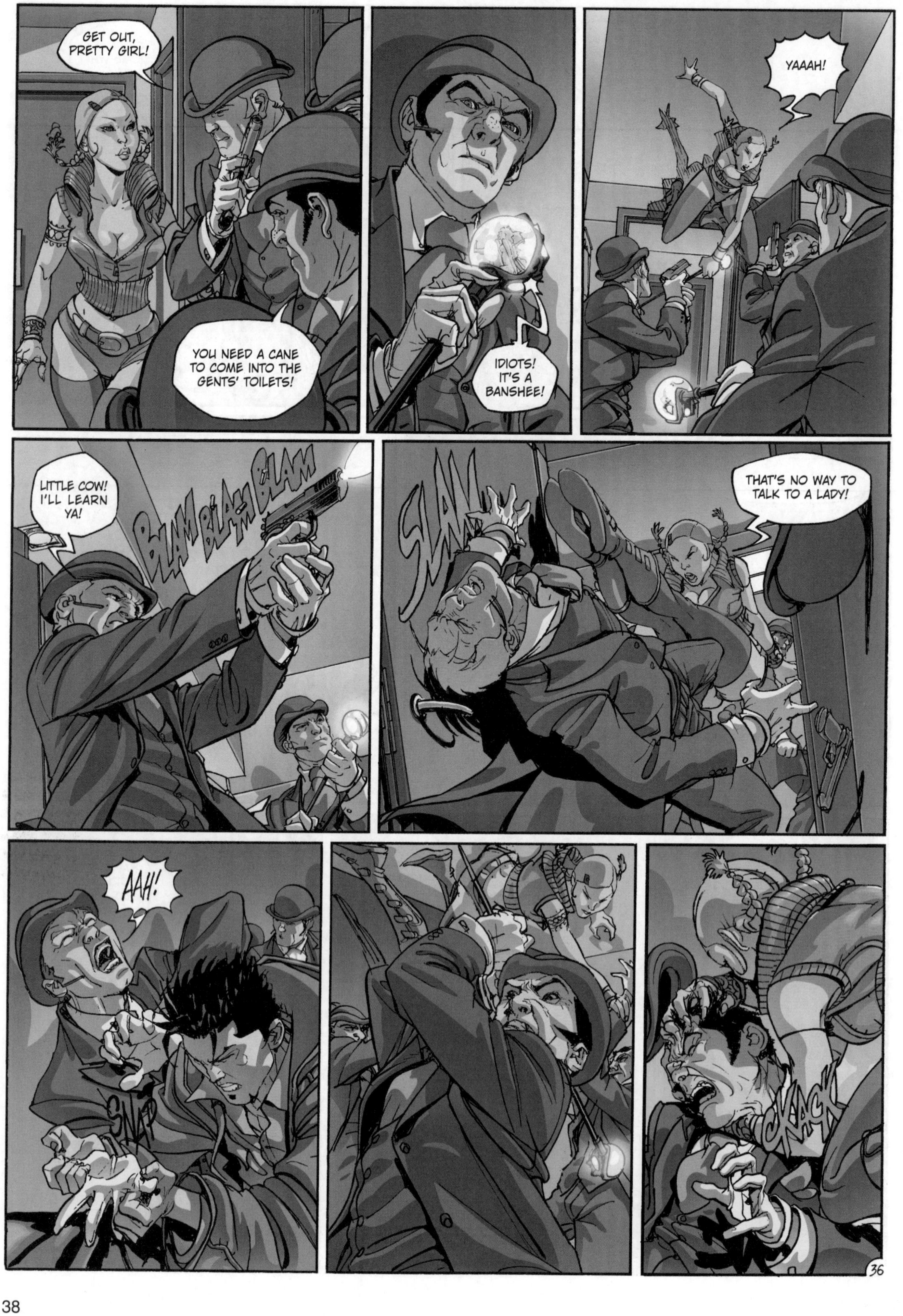
GET OUT, PRETTY GIRL!
YOU NEED A CANE TO COME INTO THE GENTS' TOILETS!
IDIOTS! IT'S A BANSHEE!
YAAAH!
LITTLE COW! I'LL LEARN YA!
BLAM BLAM BLAM
SLAM
THAT'S NO WAY TO TALK TO A LADY!
AAH!
SNAP
KRACK
36

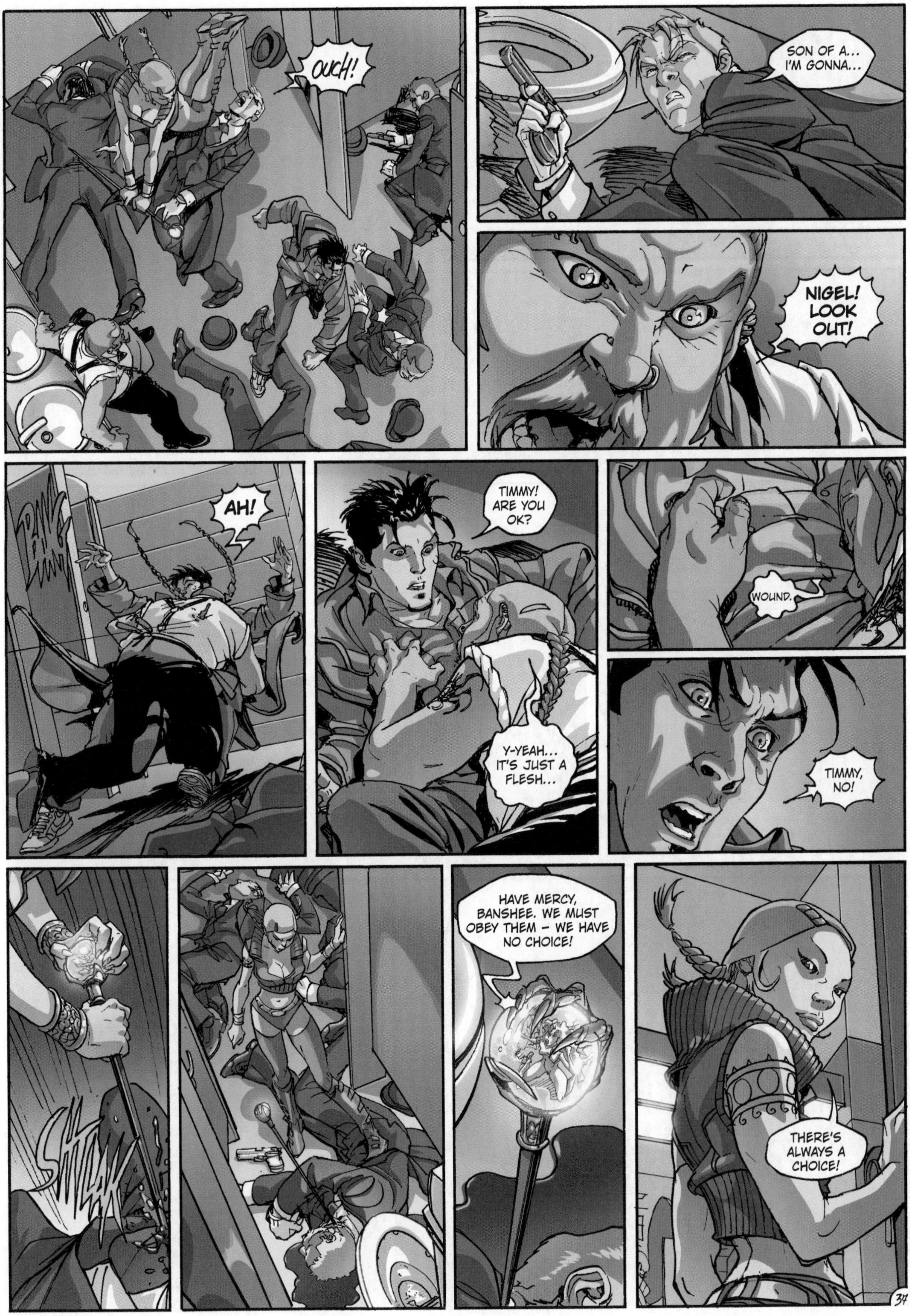
OUCH!
SON OF A... I'M GONNA...
NIGEL! LOOK OUT!
AH!
TIMMY! ARE YOU OK?
Y-YEAH... IT'S JUST A FLESH...
WOUND.
TIMMY, NO!
HAVE MERCY, BANSHEE. WE MUST OBEY THEM – WE HAVE NO CHOICE!
THERE'S ALWAYS A CHOICE!

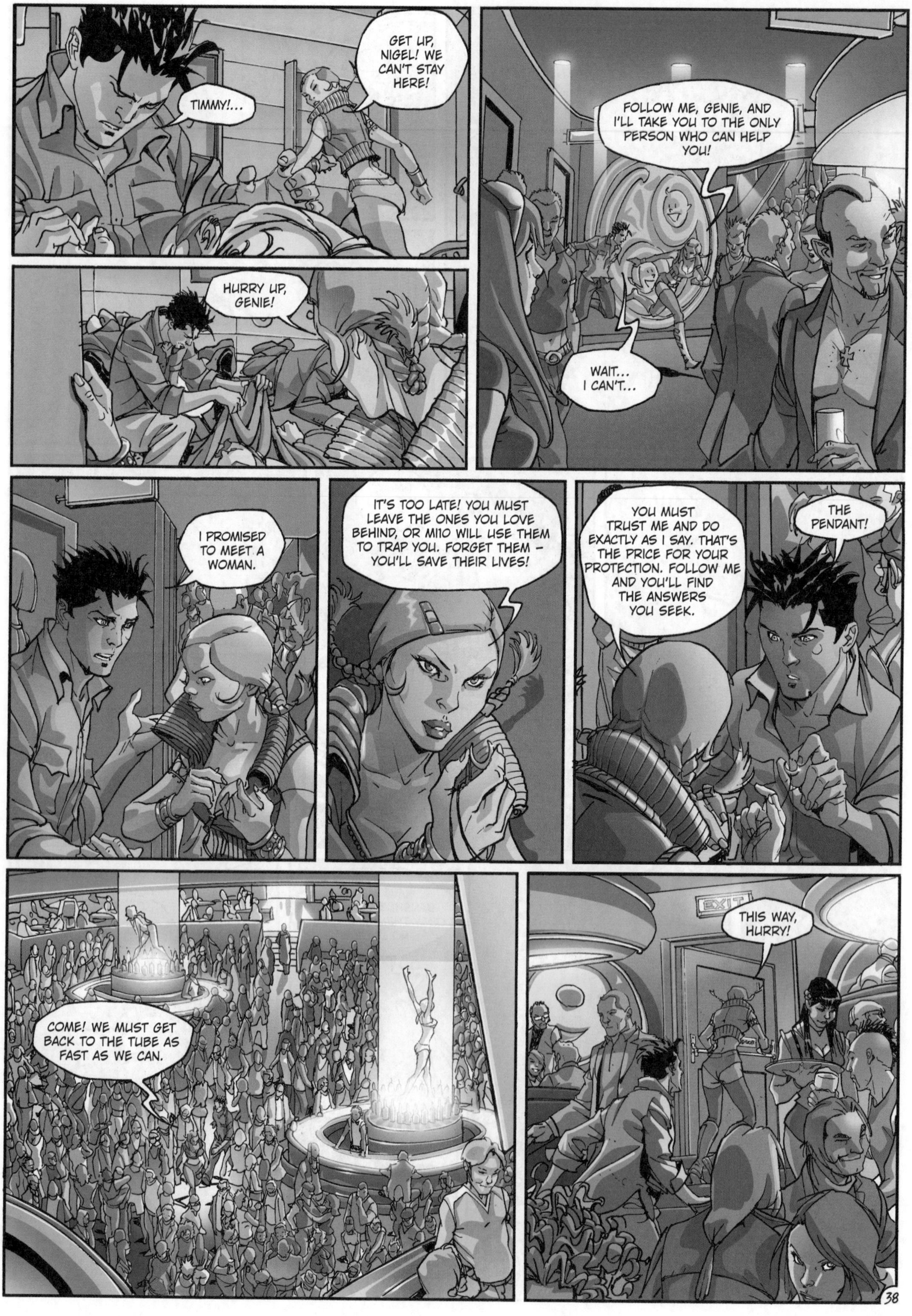

GET UP, NIGEL! WE CAN'T STAY HERE!
TIMMY!...
HURRY UP, GENIE!
FOLLOW ME, GENIE, AND I'LL TAKE YOU TO THE ONLY PERSON WHO CAN HELP YOU!
WAIT... I CAN'T...
I PROMISED TO MEET A WOMAN.
IT'S TOO LATE! YOU MUST LEAVE THE ONES YOU LOVE BEHIND, OR MI10 WILL USE THEM TO TRAP YOU. FORGET THEM – YOU'LL SAVE THEIR LIVES!
YOU MUST TRUST ME AND DO EXACTLY AS I SAY. THAT'S THE PRICE FOR YOUR PROTECTION. FOLLOW ME AND YOU'LL FIND THE ANSWERS YOU SEEK.
THE PENDANT!
COME! WE MUST GET BACK TO THE TUBE AS FAST AS WE CAN.
EXIT
THIS WAY, HURRY!
38

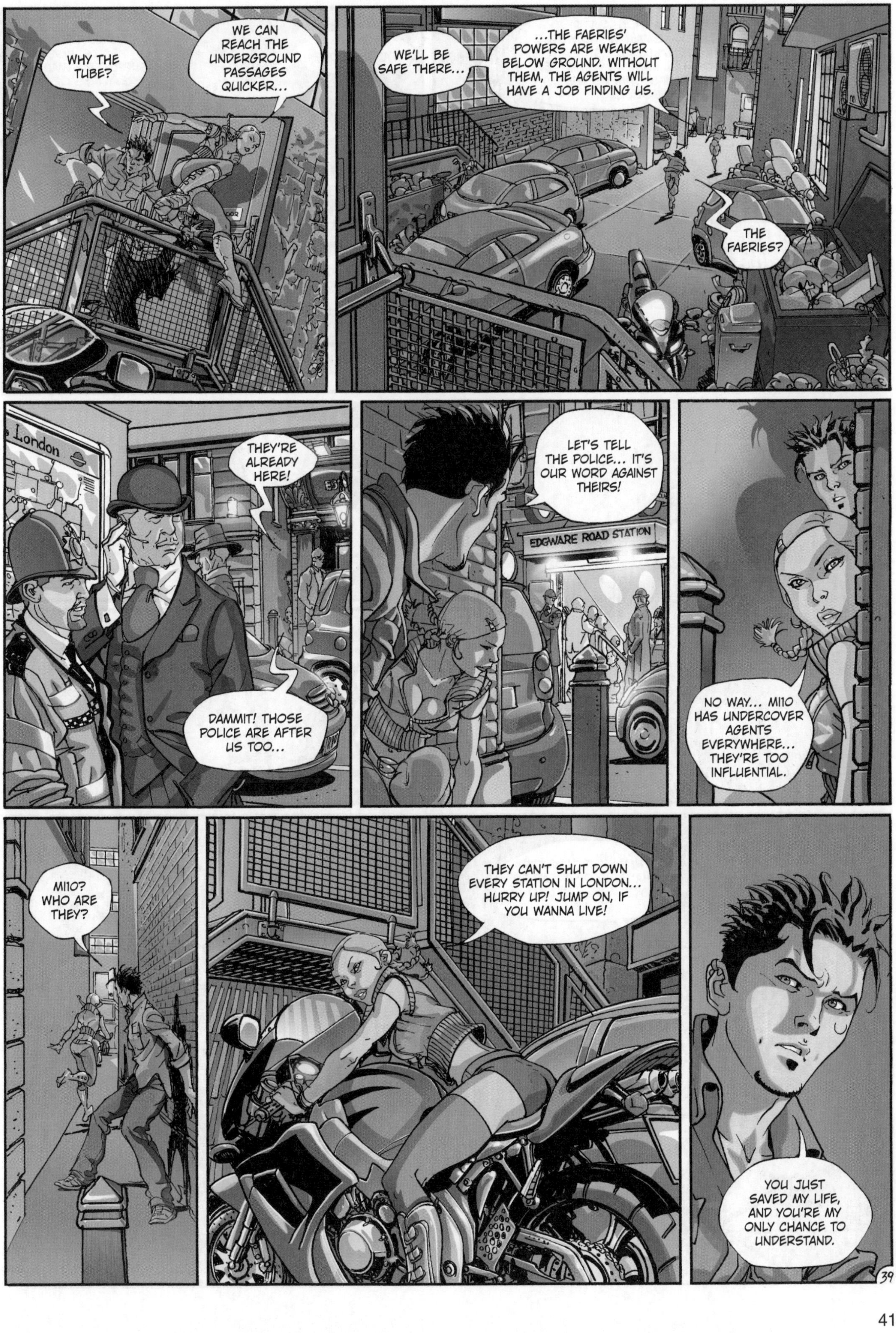
WHY THE TUBE?
WE CAN REACH THE UNDERGROUND PASSAGES QUICKER...
WE'LL BE SAFE THERE...
...THE FAERIES' POWERS ARE WEAKER BELOW GROUND. WITHOUT THEM, THE AGENTS WILL HAVE A JOB FINDING US.
THE FAERIES?
London
THEY'RE ALREADY HERE!
DAMMIT! THOSE POLICE ARE AFTER US TOO...
LET'S TELL THE POLICE... IT'S OUR WORD AGAINST THEIRS!
EDGWARE ROAD STATION
NO WAY... MI10 HAS UNDERCOVER AGENTS EVERYWHERE... THEY'RE TOO INFLUENTIAL.
MI10? WHO ARE THEY?
THEY CAN'T SHUT DOWN EVERY STATION IN LONDON... HURRY UP! JUMP ON, IF YOU WANNA LIVE!
YOU JUST SAVED MY LIFE, AND YOU'RE MY ONLY CHANCE TO UNDERSTAND.
39

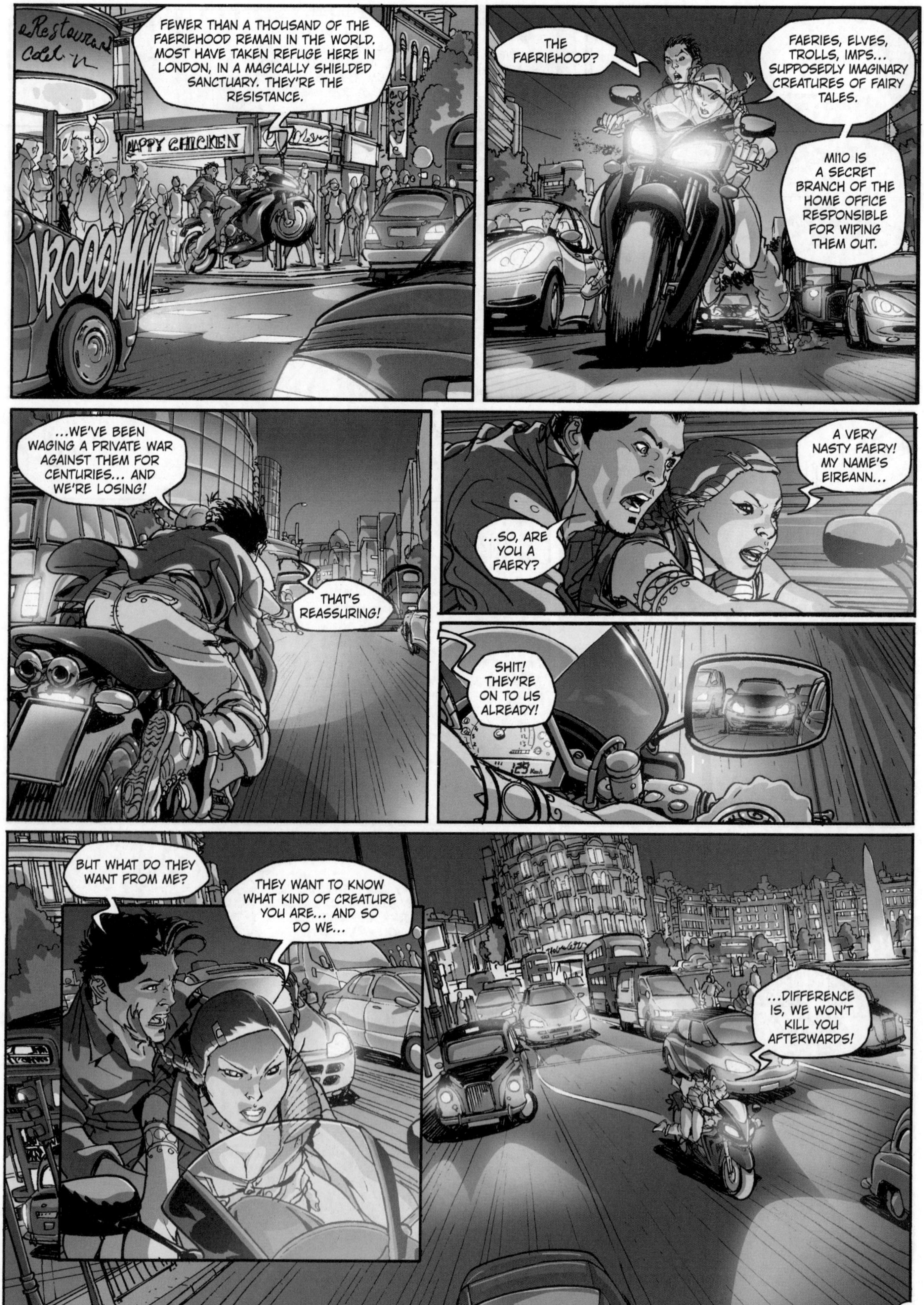
FEWER THAN A THOUSAND OF THE FAERIEHOOD REMAIN IN THE WORLD. MOST HAVE TAKEN REFUGE HERE IN LONDON, IN A MAGICALLY SHIELDED SANCTUARY. THEY'RE THE RESISTANCE.
HAPPY CHICKEN
VROOOMM
THE FAERIEHOOD?
FAERIES, ELVES, TROLLS, IMPS... SUPPOSEDLY IMAGINARY CREATURES OF FAIRY TALES.
MI10 IS A SECRET BRANCH OF THE HOME OFFICE RESPONSIBLE FOR WIPING THEM OUT.
...WE'VE BEEN WAGING A PRIVATE WAR AGAINST THEM FOR CENTURIES... AND WE'RE LOSING!
THAT'S REASSURING!
...SO, ARE YOU A FAERY?
A VERY NASTY FAERY! MY NAME'S EIREANN...
SHIT! THEY'RE ON TO US ALREADY!
BUT WHAT DO THEY WANT FROM ME?
THEY WANT TO KNOW WHAT KIND OF CREATURE YOU ARE... AND SO DO WE...
...DIFFERENCE IS, WE WON'T KILL YOU AFTERWARDS!
40

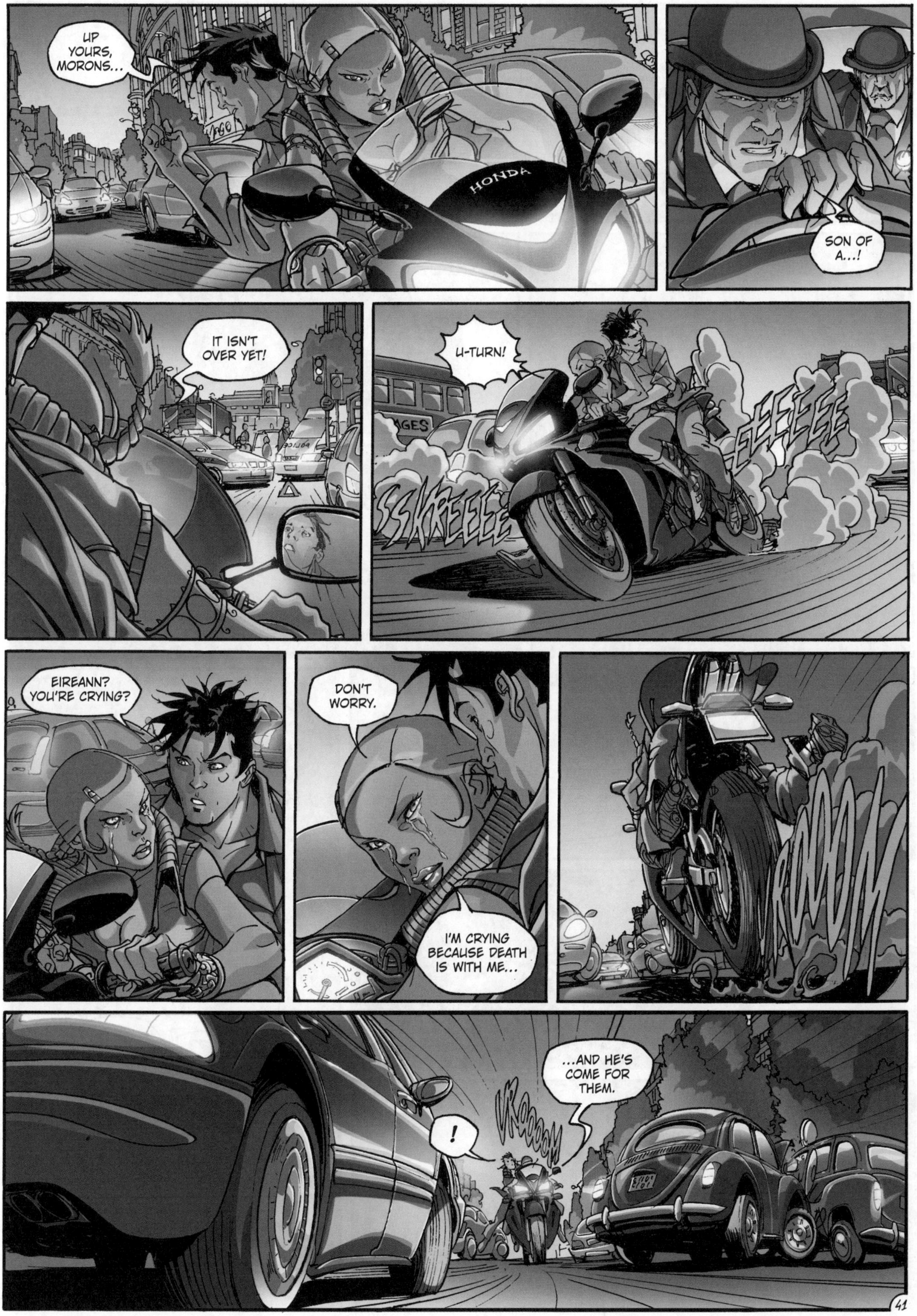
UP YOURS, MORONS...
HONDA
SON OF A...!
IT ISN'T OVER YET!
U-TURN!
SSKREEEEE
EEEEEE
EIREANN? YOU'RE CRYING?
DON'T WORRY.
I'M CRYING BECAUSE DEATH IS WITH ME...
RROOOOM
...AND HE'S COME FOR THEM.
!
VROOOOOM
41

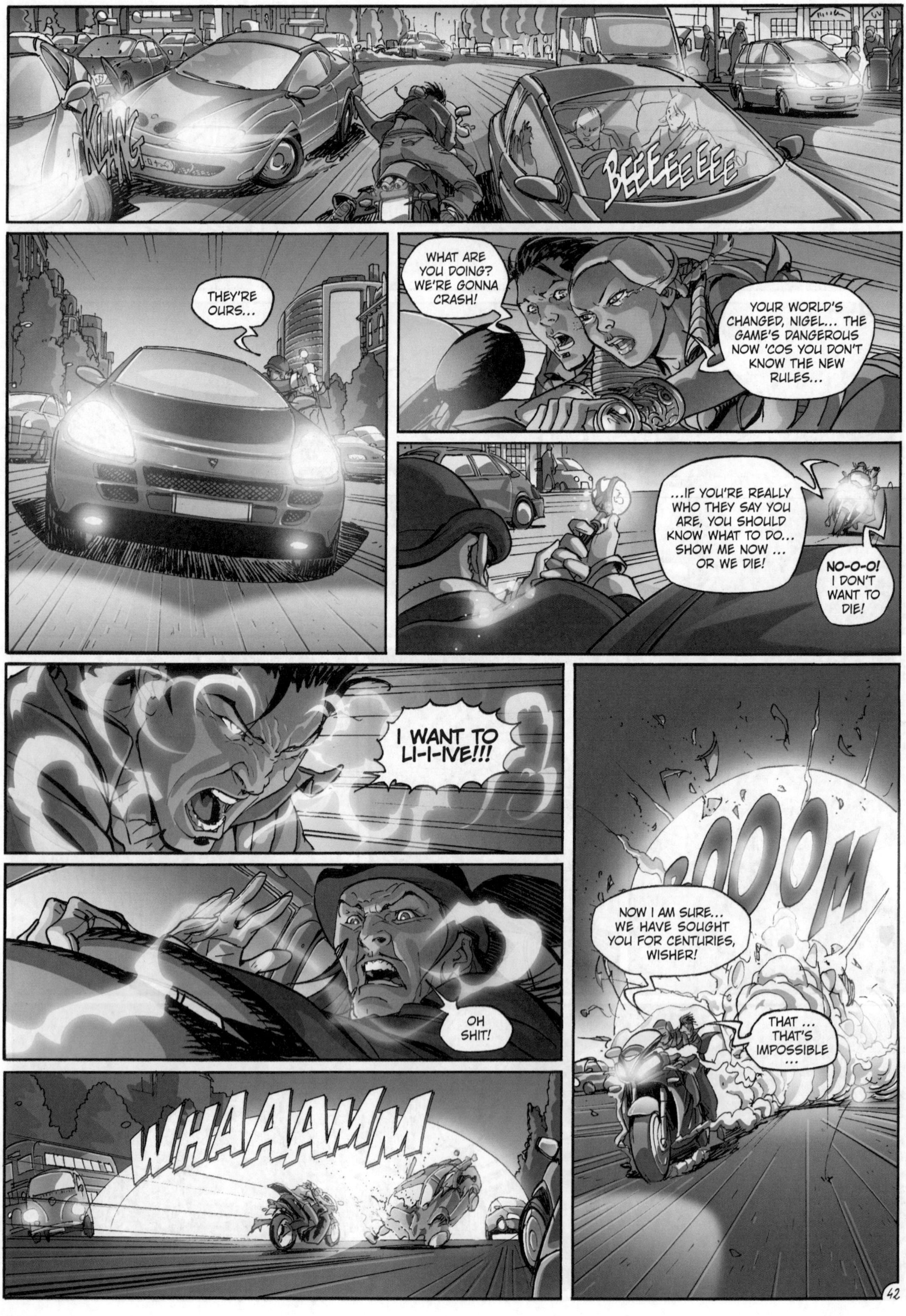
KLANG
BEEEEEEEE
THEY'RE OURS...
WHAT ARE YOU DOING? WE'RE GONNA CRASH!
YOUR WORLD'S CHANGED, NIGEL... THE GAME'S DANGEROUS NOW 'COS YOU DON'T KNOW THE NEW RULES...
...IF YOU'RE REALLY WHO THEY SAY YOU ARE, YOU SHOULD KNOW WHAT TO DO... SHOW ME NOW ... OR WE DIE!
NO-O-O! I DON'T WANT TO DIE!
I WANT TO LI-I-IVE!!!
OH SHIT!
WHAAAMM
BOOOM
NOW I AM SURE... WE HAVE SOUGHT YOU FOR CENTURIES, WISHER!
THAT ... THAT'S IMPOSSIBLE ...
42

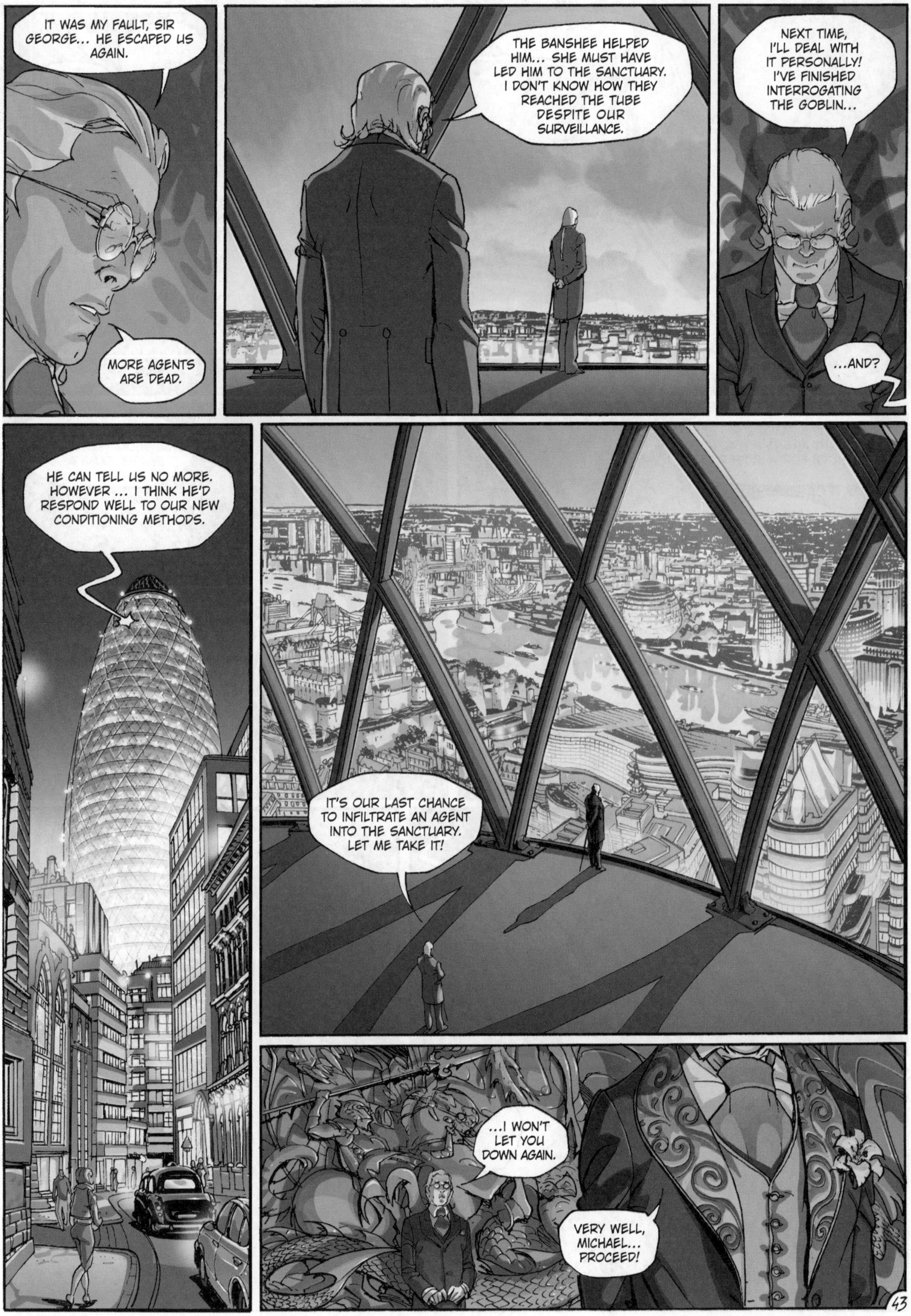
IT WAS MY FAULT, SIR GEORGE... HE ESCAPED US AGAIN.
MORE AGENTS ARE DEAD.
THE BANSHEE HELPED HIM... SHE MUST HAVE LED HIM TO THE SANCTUARY. I DON'T KNOW HOW THEY REACHED THE TUBE DESPITE OUR SURVEILLANCE.
NEXT TIME, I'LL DEAL WITH IT PERSONALLY! I'VE FINISHED INTERROGATING THE GOBLIN...
...AND?
HE CAN TELL US NO MORE. HOWEVER ... I THINK HE'D RESPOND WELL TO OUR NEW CONDITIONING METHODS.
IT'S OUR LAST CHANCE TO INFILTRATE AN AGENT INTO THE SANCTUARY. LET ME TAKE IT!
...I WON'T LET YOU DOWN AGAIN.
VERY WELL, MICHAEL... PROCEED!
43

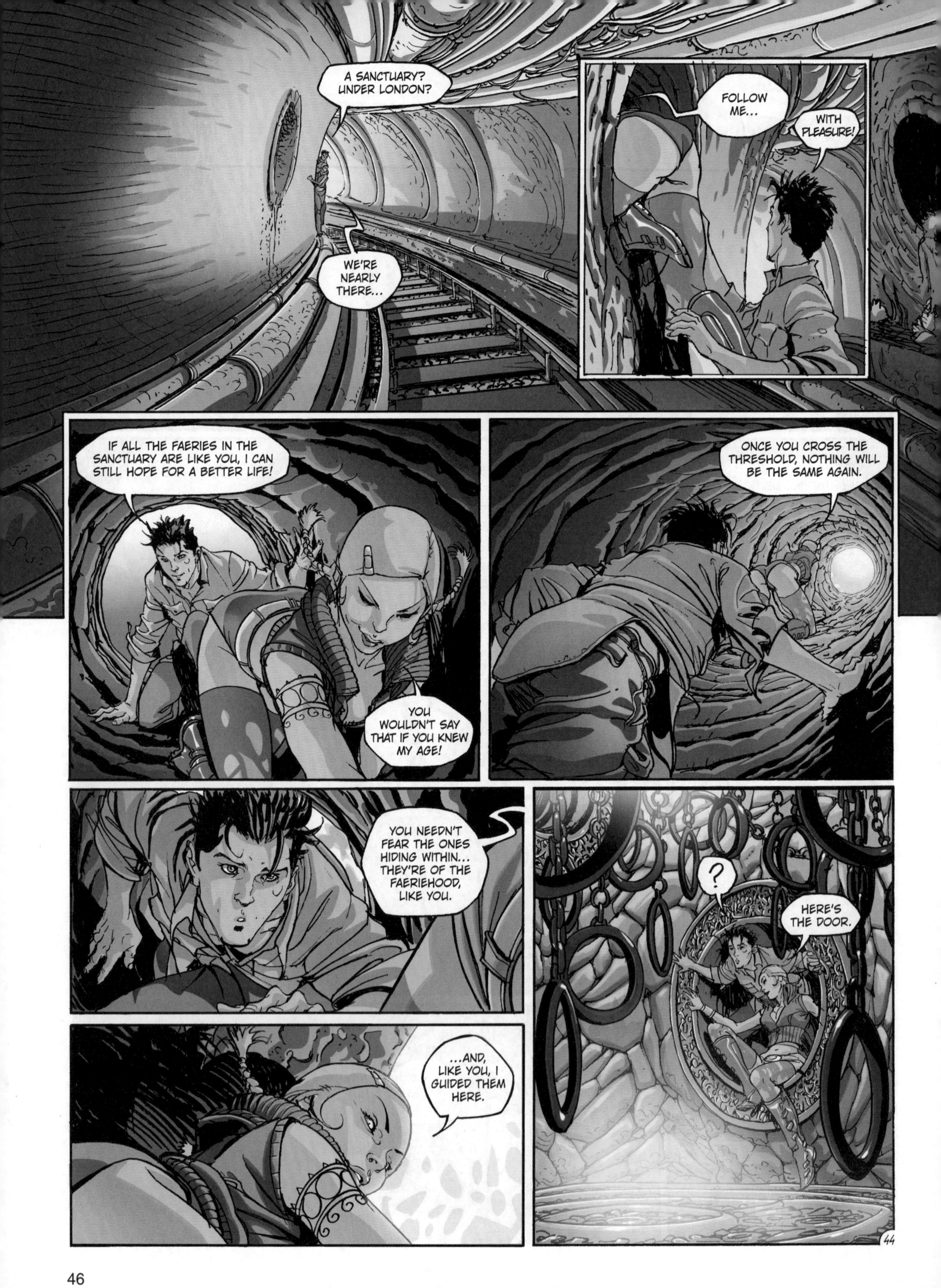
A SANCTUARY? UNDER LONDON?
WE'RE NEARLY THERE...
FOLLOW ME...
WITH PLEASURE!
IF ALL THE FAERIES IN THE SANCTUARY ARE LIKE YOU, I CAN STILL HOPE FOR A BETTER LIFE!
YOU WOULDN'T SAY THAT IF YOU KNEW MY AGE!
ONCE YOU CROSS THE THRESHOLD, NOTHING WILL BE THE SAME AGAIN.
YOU NEEDN'T FEAR THE ONES HIDING WITHIN... THEY'RE OF THE FAERIEHOOD, LIKE YOU.
...AND, LIKE YOU, I GUIDED THEM HERE.
?
HERE'S THE DOOR.
44

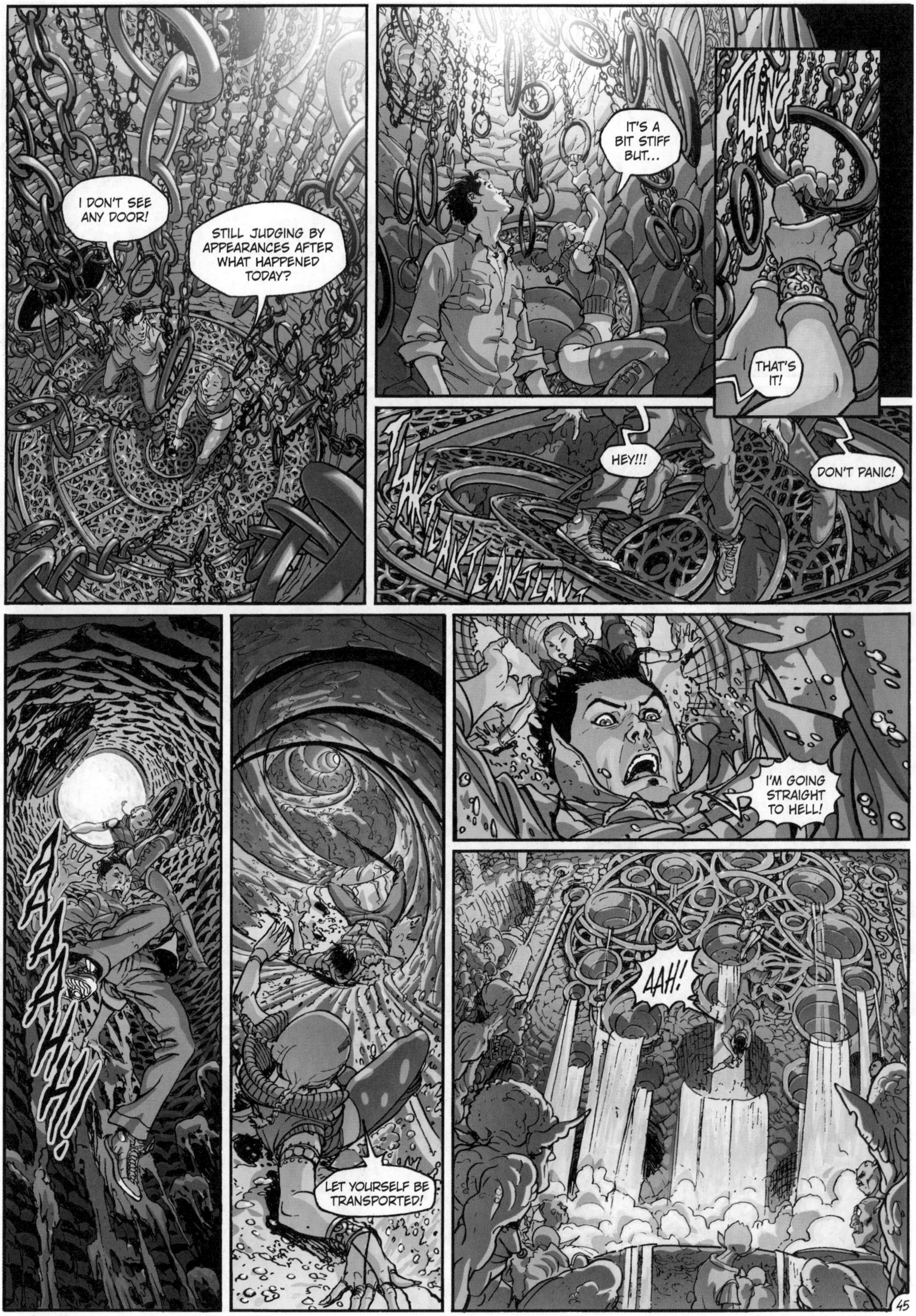
I DON'T SEE ANY DOOR!
STILL JUDGING BY APPEARANCES AFTER WHAT HAPPENED TODAY?
IT'S A BIT STIFF BUT...
THAT'S IT!
HEY!!!
DON'T PANIC!
AAAAHHH!
LET YOURSELF BE TRANSPORTED!
I'M GOING STRAIGHT TO HELL!
AAH!
45

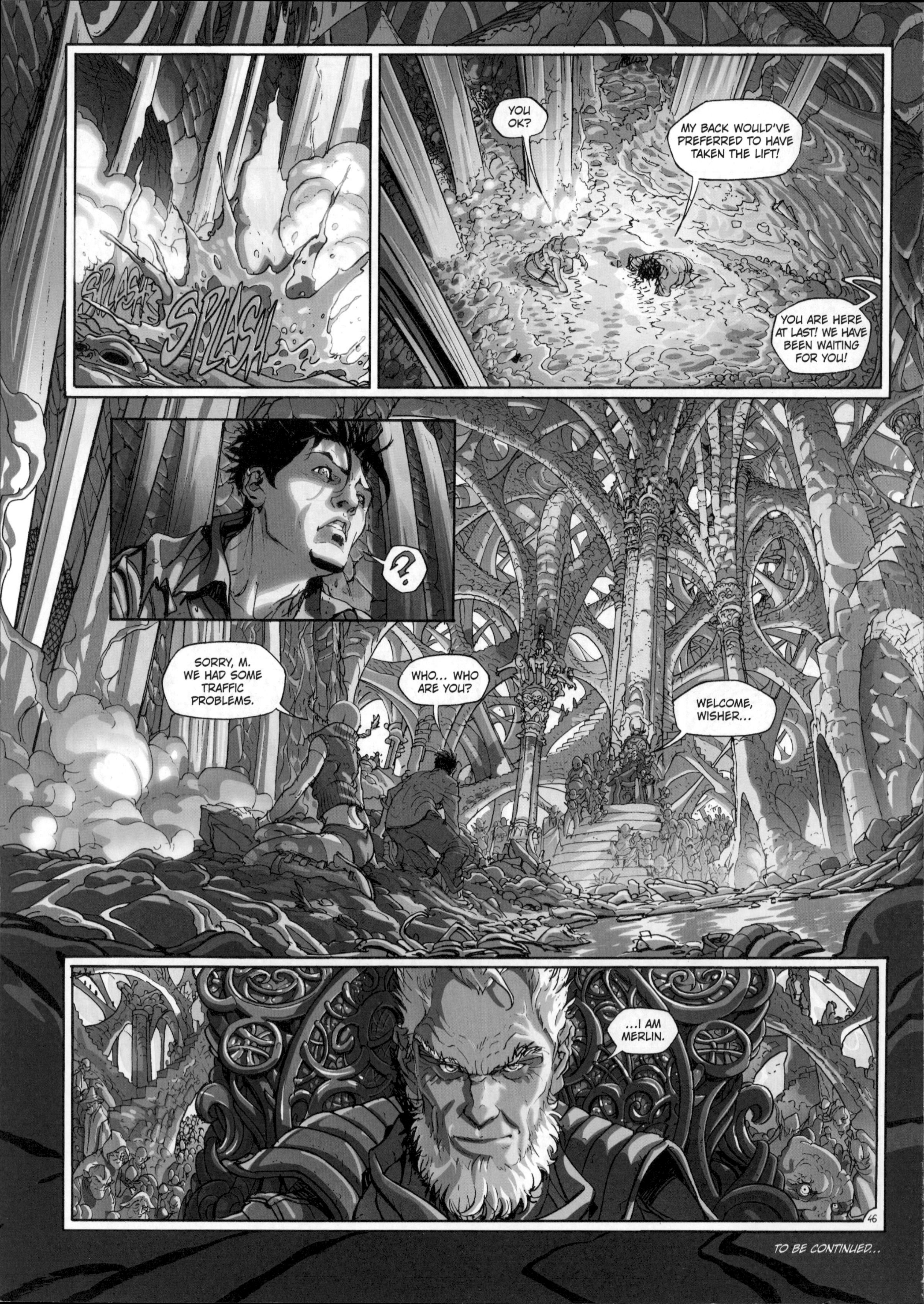
SPLASH!
SPLASH!
YOU OK?
MY BACK WOULD'VE PREFERRED TO HAVE TAKEN THE LIFT!
YOU ARE HERE AT LAST! WE HAVE BEEN WAITING FOR YOU!
?
SORRY, M. WE HAD SOME TRAFFIC PROBLEMS.
WHO... WHO ARE YOU?
WELCOME, WISHER...
...I AM MERLIN.
46
TO BE CONTINUED...